Sacred Gardens

Michel & Judy Marcellot

Schiffer Publishing Ltd®

4880 Lower Valley Road Atglen, Pennsylvania 19310

MW01170294

Copyright © 2007 by Michel and Judy Marcellot
Library of Congress Control Number: 2007926256

All rights reserved. No part of this work may be reproduced or used in any form or by any means—graphic, electronic, or mechanical, including photocopying or information storage and retrieval systems—without written permission from the publisher.

The scanning, uploading and distribution of this book or any part thereof via the Internet or via any other means without the permission of the publisher is illegal and punishable by law. Please purchase only authorized editions and do not participate in or encourage the electronic piracy of copyrighted materials.

"Schiffer," "Schiffer Publishing Ltd. & Design," and the "Design of pen and ink well" are registered trademarks of Schiffer Publishing Ltd.

All photos not marked as "Courtesy of..." are Copyrighted © Michel Marcellot

Designed by John P. Cheek
Cover design by Bruce Waters
Type set in Papyrus LET/Adobe Jensen Pro

ISBN: 978-0-7643-2724-7

Printed in China

Published by Schiffer Publishing Ltd.
4880 Lower Valley Road
Atglen, PA 19310
Phone: (610) 593-1777; Fax: (610) 593-2002
E-mail: Info@schifferbooks.com

For the largest selection of fine reference books on this and related subjects, please visit our web site at **www.schifferbooks.com**
We are always looking for people to write books on new and related subjects. If you have an idea for a book please contact us at the above address.

This book may be purchased from the publisher.
Include $3.95 for shipping.
Please try your bookstore first.
You may write for a free catalog.

In Europe, Schiffer books are distributed by
Bushwood Books
6 Marksbury Ave.
Kew Gardens
Surrey TW9 4JF England
Phone: 44 (0) 20 8392-8585; Fax: 44 (0) 20 8392-9876
E-mail: info@bushwoodbooks.co.uk
Website: www.bushwoodbooks.co.uk
Free postage in the U.K., Europe; air mail at cost.

Contents

Acknowledgements

We would like to extend our sincere gratitude to everyone who contributed to the making of this book:

Thank you, Schiffer Publishing and our Editors, Tina Skinner and Dinah Roseberry, who seemed to trust us to actually do this right.

Thank you, Jessie Turbayne, who insisted we write a book and then showed us how to actually do it. (You scared Judy a little bit but she recovered.) Thanks to our neighbor and friend, Grammy nominee (his aunt says that means he lost), Todd Urbonos, and to Martha and Bill Rice, more neighbors and friends who jumped right in anytime we asked them for help.

Thank you to our amazing and beautiful staff at Seven Arrows who took charge and did a better job at running the store and nursery than we do—Pettina Harden, Mary Blue, Kate Merrill, Mary Tuomisto, Debbie Bergh and Sue Allaire. Special thanks to Pettina and Debbie for their über organizational systems to keep all the photographers straight. Dave Erwin and Claudia Binns, your friendship, encouragement and uncensored critique has been invaluable!

A special "Thank you" to Dr. Leo Kadanoff and Dr. Robert Schoch who generously gave their time to meet with Michel and help him make sense of the garden, from a non-gardening perspective. Special thanks to Dr. Fred Meli's insightful comments about the origins of sacred landscapes.

And a very special "We are in your debt" kind of "thank you" to the incredibly generous photographers who shared their amazing pictures: Alan & Elizabeth Taylor, Alice Stahl, Anna Rosinska, Anne Bowerman, Bill Adams, Bill Norris, Brent Olson, Carolyn Heathcote, Chanda Star DeMartini, Cosmic Fusion Photography, Darlene Greydanus, David Stephensen, Desmond Cannon, Doug Greene, Eric Heupel, M. Fleur-Ange Lamothe, Florence Blanchetierre, Gerald Deschenes, Mike Wong, Nancy Foote, Nicole Simoes, Paul Moody, Remy Omar, Rob Corbett, Robert Schoch, Robyn Alvin, Rodd Halstead Photography, Sheila Quonoey, Sheila Bocchine, Stella McLoughlin, Tim Valentine, Yolanda Molina, Laura S. Kicey, Rafael Fernandez Leiro, Sandra Serretti, Giorgio Castellini, Hanaan Rosenthal, Heidi Noëlle Schachtschneider, Ian Wright, Irene Suchocki, Jacques Bauer, Javier Esteban Sepulveda, Jean Simard, Jim Evans, Johanne Rosenthal, John Mewitt, John Suler, Jonny Baker, Katie Tarpey, Liz Kearley, Lenny Zimmerman, Lucas Foglia Photography, Mary A. Smith, Mel Cameron Radford, Michelle Pitt, Marcel More, Danya Martin, Stewart Martin, Wendy Purdy, Rick Wheelock, Anita Tieleman, Valerianna Claff, Michael Oberman.

All photographs are used with the permission of the photographers. The authors claim no responsibility for misidentification of photograph ownership and/or copyright infringements.

And, of course, a huge thank you to the gardeners who shared their stories and provided much of the inspiration found in the book: Gerry and Lea Deschenes, Valerianna Claff, Jan Hindley, Jenna Greene, Linda Dowd, Sue and Steve Burek, Liz Cantrell, Thea Alvin, Margaret Alicea, John Fazzino, Nancy Foote, Johanne Rosenthal, Phil Edmonds, Sheila Quonoey, Barbara Gee, Katherine Brown, Sheila Bocchine, and Heidi Noelle Schachtschneider.

"As for garden photographers, how differently they see things. With what ease the camera seems to compose a picture of great beauty with its discriminating lens. The naked eye can't censor some ugly sight on the periphery of vision; the photographer takes the perfect shot and picks for us just what we need to see."

—Mirabel Osler

What We Did and Didn't Want

When we were approached to write this book, we gave a lot of thought to what *we* would like to read about the subject. We read lots of books, or at least *parts* of lots of books about "spiritual gardening," "sacred gardens," and the like. We knew we wanted ordinary people to be inspired by the stories of other "ordinary" people. We wanted people to look at the pictures and think, "I can do that. That would look good in my garden."

We looked at pictures of absolutely stunning gardens that had been created as spiritual works of art. How could one not be struck by the awesome beauty of England's Prince Charles' "Carpet Garden" based in style and color on an oriental rug owned by the Prince, for example? But, you couldn't really reproduce it yourself, could you? In addition to never really figuring out how to address a prince in a letter (we thought we might be given some leeway, here, being American and unwise in the ways of protocol and good manners), we decided not to focus on the gardens of the rich and famous. It also seemed to us that some of these gardens appeared to be void of emotion, that is, they didn't appear to reflect the emotional makeup or character of the person who lived there. We could be completely wrong about this, clearly not being acquainted with the rich and famous residents of these perfect gardens. Maybe they reflect the precise characters of the residents.

So, the book took off on its own, with "ordinary" gardeners like us popping up everywhere.

The world probably doesn't need another gardening book. And a book professing connection with spirituality, well, it's probably all been said as well. We also struggled with the word "spiritual." If the same source energy flows through all things, as we think it does, how do you separate the spiritual from the non-spiritual? By judging what we designate "good" as spiritual and the things we call "bad" as non-spiritual? There's clearly no universally accepted definitions of "good" and "bad"—just look around the world and see how quickly that becomes obvious. So that didn't work for us. A landscape designer friend of ours considers himself an atheist. But he loves plants with a *capital L*, and his work, particularly his home garden, "feels" full of this love. Not "spiritual?"

Instead, we decided to take a broader view. Could it be that when you are in love with anything—a person, your dog, your cat, your garden, an armadillo, anything at all—you are fully connected to the one force that is creating the universe? In the end, we had to let go of our previously held views of people and their paths.

It's been so darned much fun to talk with people, to photograph them and their special spaces. To write a book was just the next logical step in our own journeys. Something to do for fun. Something to share with others. What fun is doing your passion if you can't share it with others? As our journeys, both as gardeners and as human beings, have been guided and inspired by many people at various times, we hope this book may serve the same for others.

Several years ago, we made the decision that if it wasn't fun, we weren't going to do it. It took a little while for our decision to take hold and manifest as our reality, but that's often how things happen, we think. We imagine it's possible to plant a seed and have a full-grown plant the next day, but it doesn't often happen. We've read of instantaneous manifestations in books like *Behaving as if the God in All Life Mattered* and *The Magic of Findhorn*, but we've found we often have to grow into our new belief systems and new realities.

Both Judy's mother and father died within three weeks of each other in the spring of 2005. One day, soon after their passing, Judy was sitting quietly, trying to "make contact," trying to feel their presence and communicate in some way. She very clearly heard her dad say, "*Survival is not what it's cracked up to be, Judy. Go out and have more fun.*" It was not until she heard or felt these words that the decision we arrived at several years before really took hold in present day, three-dimensional reality.

And so we began having more fun. We started showing up at performances of our many musician friends. We started dancing. We started holding barn dances. One little thing led to the next. The collector plant nursery and public garden we call our business, which used to have us so tied up in knots each spring, is happily going on its merry way. It has gotten lovelier, more organized, drawing more energy to itself and putting more out.

> *"Filling up and spilling over it's an endless waterfall."*
> —Chris Williamson

People often come to our nursery and gardens to get ideas for their own spaces. Everything we've done here has been accomplished with clear intent and sweat equity. No big money. No winning the lottery. No assistance from a rich uncle. Just passion for the doing of it, joy in the moment of doing it, and gratitude to an infinite Universe that always responds "Yes."

And so we wrote a gardening book about ordinary gardeners and their connection to some larger part of the cosmos. We met some wonderful human beings and had a great time doing it. Thanks, Dad/Rick, for reminding us that life is supposed to be fun.

So, we learned to always look on the bright side of life, follow our passions, and say "thank you" a lot.

Oh, and go dancing.

Dad said, *"Survival isn't what it's cut out to be, get out and have more fun!"* The Providence Wholebellies perform at Seven Arrows.

Now on we go, as all good gardeners, planting and tending to the cosmos.

> *"Gratitude unlocks the fullness of life. It turns what we have into enough, and more. It turns denial into acceptance, chaos to order, confusion to clarity. It can turn a meal into a feast, a house into a home, a stranger into a friend. Gratitude makes sense of our past, brings peace for today, and creates a vision for tomorrow."*
> —Melody Beattie

In the Beginning

Michel's adventures in gardening began very early, springing from his intense love of all things natural. He spent most of his free time outside and found comfort in the predictability of the natural order of things, particularly when his family life was much more unpredictable. He would spend hours re-routing small streams in the woods, creating pools and waterfalls, mossy beaches and rocky outcroppings. Gradually, he turned to planting beds, building steps, creating small garden pools and experimenting with transplanting wild plants into his mom's garden. *"I used my feelings as my guide, even as a kid. How did I feel in the space? Was it easy to navigate the stairs or path? Could others join me without feeling crowded? Did I feel good? It didn't really matter what the place looked like if it didn't feel 'right', even then."*

Before we started gardening for a living, there was reading. Have you ever read a book that spoke to some part of yourself, that left you no choice but to stop what you were doing and proceed down a new path? That was the impact *The Magic of Findhorn* by Paul Hawken (the Smith and Hawken one), and *Growing Fragrant Herbs for Fun and Profit*, (a little photocopied booklet by Phyllis Shaudys) had on us. *The Magic of Findhorn*, published in 1975, told the story of the evolution of a small group of individuals (three adults and three children) living near the tiny village of Findhorn on the northern coast of Scotland. Their little group grew into a world famous spiritual community, which served as a model for many similar communities all over the world. But before that happened, they became known as consummate gardeners, transforming a small piece of seemingly inhospitable land into a world-class garden, drawing the attention of gardening experts from all over the world.

For Judy, the attraction of Findhorn was its gardens and clear articulation of the apparent relationship between the actual physical gardens and the devic or other dimensional consciousness. This seemed to include connection and communication with other dimensional forms they called devas, elementals, and nature spirits, all which resonated within us. As a little girl, Judy used to invent stories about the fairies and other little beings who would come each night and visit her in her bedroom. She can still feel the excitement their "pretend" visits brought her. At one point, she remembers telling a continuing story about the visits to her younger sister, and how the two of them could follow the fairies into their kingdom. This was accomplished by leaving the fairies some of the cut glass "jewels," from their sheriff badges, under the bed. These little trinkets would serve as some sort of payment for admission into the fairy kingdom. Judy hopes her sister has forgotten this as it was a source of resentment, and feelings of betrayal on her sister's part, when Judy felt compelled to tell her the "truth"—that she was "making up" the whole thing. At any rate, at Findhorn people actually spoke freely and often of their connection and communication with this part of creation.

When we began the nursery, a woman who claimed to talk to these other dimensional creatures would visit regularly, play her recorder in one of the greenhouses, and have animated and lively conversations with different fairies, gnomes and the like. We discovered that many books about human/nature spirit interaction had actually been written. After reading the *Magic of Findhorn*, we knew we had to follow our hearts down a new path. That was 1980. For years, Judy gardened happily, holding her own conversations with this part of creation, sometimes thinking she saw little forms of light, darting here and there. She saw them in her mind's eye with lovely diaphanous wings, in little red outfits and hats, and once, while hiking the Long Trail in Vermont, as a three-foot gnome-like gentleman who obviously, by his manner, held some authority in the fairy world. In writing this book, we encountered very respectable members of the community who fully accept the existence of this realm of consciousness. Judy is happily re-connecting with a part of her life that was joyful and lighthearted.

The other inspirational writing that pushed us down a new road was a hand-typed, photocopied booklet called *Growing Fragrant Herbs for Profit*. We contacted Phyllis Shaudys, the author, after reading about her home-based business in *The Mother Earth News*, a favorite magazine of ours at the time. Her enthusiastic "you can do anything you put your mind to" spirit led us to quit our jobs with nothing but faith in our ability to do our passion and follow our bliss. After reading Phyllis' booklet, we grew one hundred or so little herb plants and took them to a local flea market to test-market our new plan. We sold maybe a dozen plants, pronounced our test a success and decided to open a real business! And no, we were not under the influence of any funny stuff. Our delusions and illusions were completely of our own making. We went on to selling from a lean-to tent in the driveway, and branched out to fairs and festivals.

In the beginning, people had no idea what to do with the beautiful little potted herbs we were offering. Our booths at the fairs and festivals were always beautiful, fragrant affairs, but the folks selling soda bottles with colored sand were the ones raking in the dollars. Herbs were just beginning to enjoy a renaissance in popularity. People were only starting to incorporate herbs in cooking, replacing that great American flavor enhancer, salt. People were beginning to look at herbal medicine as a viable health alternative. In addition, herbal wreaths and fragrant crafts were enjoying great popularity as well. Little by little our business started to grow.

About the same time, we went to see a business counselor at a well-known organization of retired businesspersons who offer advice to new business people. A very nice man told us our chosen careers would make a great hobby business, but one of us should get a real job to support ourselves. A few years later, one of the group's representatives called us to ask our advice on similar new businesses they were advising.

Over the years, we have been desperately broke (can't really say "poor" because we were grateful for so much of what we did have—the opportunity to work together, being part of each seasonal change, being around the kids and lots more). We've also been well off, and everything in between. Like the so-called Butterfly Effect (a metaphor which says that if a butterfly flaps its wings in the Amazon basin, a chain of intimately connected events result in say, a hurricane, somewhere else on the planet), we discovered the interconnectedness of all things. All things cause all things.

> *"There is a calmness to a life lived in gratitude, a quiet joy."*
> —Ralph H. Blum

You Are Where You Are and the Universe Lets You Know It

All sorts of esoteric philosophies speak to the thought that, at any given time, human beings are third dimensional expressions of their thoughts and feelings—physical representations of vibrational energy. We have not come to the place where we find ourselves in each moment by accident, but rather as a result of the dominant vibration we are emitting, the drumbeat we have been beating by the choices we make in every moment.

> *"The human doesn't see things as they are, but as he is."*
> —Racter

We each had difficult life-long relationships with members of our respective families and had just begun our healing processes with counseling and all kinds of alternative healing modalities. Because some of our family members were rather conspicuous consumers, we somehow decided that affluence must impact you in a negative way. (In other words, money was the root of all evil.) So, we decided that the less money we had, the more authentic, kind, and considerate people we would be. We thought true service could only be performed by the Mother Theresas of the world—in simplicity and the non-accumulation of earthly goods. We took the oil heater out of the house and used only the three working fireplaces to keep us warm through record (of course) cold New England winters. We sold our beautiful, brand new truck and bought a beat up *VW* bus, which promptly fell apart, and became the first in a series of similar vehicles. And we decided that to be good, spiritual people performing a service to the world, we needed to be "serious" as well as poor. We threw away the collection of vinyl 45s Judy had collected during an earlier series of trips to Jamaica with former Peace Corp friends. She even tossed Buddy Holly's first hit on vinyl. Michel had a great collection of newer reggae albums. Out it all went. Into the dumpster with everything! Only Gregorian chants and classical music for us.

Our daughters came to live with us during this period. We met the Hmong in the early 1970s just as they were beginning to arrive as refugees from war-torn Indo-China. Judy was still directing the agency she founded, which provided English as a Second Language classes to adult immigrants. One particular agency grant targeted recent Vietnamese, Hmong, Lao, and Cambodian refugees who came to Providence, Rhode Island by way of the refugee camps in Thailand. In the late 1970s, we were vegetable gardening and not much else. The Hmong were an agricultural people in their homeland in the mountains of Laos. Their agrarian slash and burn, shamanistic lifestyle fascinated us and we grew close to a lot of the adult students and their families. At one point, we offered the use of some of our land to anyone who wanted to plant it. Several extended families took us up on the offer and raised beds thick with tomatoes, squashes, cucumbers, and greens grew up in our backfields. We loved walking through the beds and meeting gardeners of all ages from toddlers to old folk. We started attending all sorts of Hmong celebrations in nearby Providence, not understanding too much, but enjoying the energy of large families working together with everyone occupied—like some sort of a well-oiled machine with a certain amount of chaos thrown in. It was impressive to see how a people who had lost so much of their underlying identification through horror and hardship, regrouped to create a new version of their lives.

The Hmong tribe from the northern hills of Laos brought a rich mythology to their new country. Southside Community Gardens Providence, Rhode Island. *Courtesy of Lucas Foglia Photography*

Courtesy of Lucas Foglia Photography

Gardening is a large part of the Hmong tribal identity. Southside Community Gardens Providence, Rhode Island. *Courtesy of Lucas Foglia Photography*

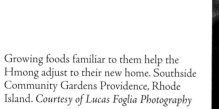

Growing foods familiar to them help the Hmong adjust to their new home. Southside Community Gardens Providence, Rhode Island. *Courtesy of Lucas Foglia Photography*

One day, Yer, the father of one the gardening families, came to us with a question: *"Would you take one or two of my daughters to live with you for a year or two, or maybe the rest of their lives?"* The Hmong live in extended family networks, clans, and in their pre-war peaceful agrarian communities, this arrangement wasn't that strange to them. We don't know why, but it never sounded strange to us either. *"Sure,"* we said. A ceremony was held in which we think we were *sort of* adopted into the clan, but we're not completely certain. There was a lot of ritual drinking, toasts, and advice. The girls were too little (six and seven) to know what was being said, and to this day, although bilingual in Spanish and French, we have learned very little Hmong, we are ashamed to say. After each long oration, our translator would turn to us and say, *"He says good luck."* That began a life-long association with members of the Kue and Hang clans that continues to this day, although not in as intense a form as it was when the girls were little and the families lived fifteen minutes away.

In order to care for Yer's daughters, we had to be inducted into their family's clan. At least that's what we *think* happened! *Courtesy of Lucas Foglia Photography*

Foua and True lived with us during the week and went home for the weekends and summer vacations to Providence. We experienced the things "normal" families do, except our family was much larger, and very diverse viewpoints had to be honored. For instance, when the girls were little, Sheng, their mom, asked us not to let them play outside at dusk, as that was a time when spirits might come and cause the girls to become sick. The mind is such a big part of creating one's reality—who were we to say that this couldn't happen? Although there are huge parts of the Hmong culture we will probably never really understand because of the language barrier, we expanded our acceptance of things "seen" and "unseen". So the girls didn't leave the house at dusk.

Shamanic healing, too, was a big part of our expanded views. When the girls got sick, the shaman was called in and a ceremony performed. The girls also saw western doctors. Although we were perfectly willing to try herbal remedies first, they took an awful lot of antibiotics as children. It was important for their families to adapt to the ways of the current country of residence. So they thought. At least, so *we* thought they thought. The shaman was also called in for any emotional crisis, and ceremonies were held for a wide spectrum of issues. Often, if the girls misbehaved, we had family meetings with the offender and four adults. When the girls became teenagers, they were needed back at home to help with the younger children.

People often ask us, "How can you raise children and then give them up?" For us, it was a great illustration of the fact that your children never really "belong" to you anyway. Other parents may have to learn this the hard way. For us, it was the natural order of things. Our kids really didn't belong to us! By the late 1980s, many of the Hmong had resettled in North Carolina and California. In 1991, our extended family moved to Minnesota to join other clan members who had resettled there. They were able to buy cheap land to farm. Sheng and Yer refer to us as "sister" and "brother," and although our relationship was closer when the family lived in nearby Providence, we refer to the girls as our kids and Sheng and Yer as their "natural parents." Life with the girls was wonderful.

The rest of our lives was all about the suffering. So, in addition to aestheticism, we subscribed to the whole suffering paradigm as well. True service to the world, we thought, was all about suffering. One had to suffer to grow and "learn your lessons" which implied we were somehow insufficient, ignorant, or broken as we were. But the suffering should be only temporary, we thought. If we did all sorts of good things now, we would be rewarded with our hearts' desires at some future time. Suffer now; reap the rewards at some future time. Sort of pay now, collect later. We discovered there were a few inherent problems with this line of thought, however. Who decides when you've suffered enough, for instance? Who decides what you're supposed to learn? How do you know if you've actually learned your lesson? Is there a grading system? And what about the rewards? Who decides what they are and makes sure you get them? When could we expect to see the rewards in this *pay now, collect later* plan? At first, we went along our way merely suffering from circumstances we chose. Later, circumstances we never would have chosen in a million years started showing up in our lives. Voluntary aestheticism turned into involuntary poverty. We lived hand to mouth, loaded with debt from living on credit cards during the winter months when the nursery was closed and paying the cards off in the spring in the best-case scenario, (no excessive rain on spring weekends and no drought during the rest of the summer). We planted some beginner type herb gardens in raised beds that were okay but nothing to write home about, although people came to photograph them anyway. Outer reflected inner.

> "Every natural fact is a symbol of some spiritual fact."
> —Ralph Waldo Emerson

The Chinese art of Feng Shui speaks to this, as well, of course. Certain energy flows result in certain physical manifestations. Change the energy flow and change the manifestation. Obviously, this is an extreme simplification of the philosophy behind the practice, but it seemed to bear out for us when we consulted a Feng Shui practitioner for both our home and business, located on the same property. Stanley, our Feng Shui consultant, actually told us we shouldn't be living in the house at all. (It's a 1790s Cape with tiny rooms and low, slanted ceilings.) But as we had no money to buy another property, and we had invested all our money and a huge amount of sweat equity into the farm and nursery, moving was not an option for us. We were in a "low cash flow phase" of our lives to boot. You may translate that as "broke." However, there was a list of physical changes we could make with the house that would help.

So we went ahead and knocked down walls, opened the front door, which we had nailed shut for some reason—just another unfinished project, we think—and did everything else Stanley recommended. Immediately, we saw changes manifest in the physical. We received three unexpected deliveries of an organic mulch, which we sold wholesale to other nurseries and, because of that, were able to live comfortably the rest of the winter. That was pretty neat, we thought! Stanley also told us that, as we made changes to the house, we would work through some of our other issues in life as well—things we had carried around from childhood, and that affected our lives and the way we looked at things and operated in the world. We were all for *that*. "*Change your environment*," he said, "*and change yourselves*." That seemed easy.

But easier *said* than done. There certainly appeared to be a connection between the state of the house and gardens and our emotional lives. In other words, our outer world always appeared to mirror our emotional worlds. When we were broke and depressed, the house and gardens were lackluster, ordinary, and uninspiring. Although the gardens were photographed for a book and several magazines at the time, we saw their potential to be something much more and didn't really see them as attractive. We definitely saw the connection between our emotional states of being and the shape of the gardens and nursery. As we grew, changed, and began healing ourselves of the emotional baggage we carried around, the gardens became more vibrant and problem areas resolved themselves. But this didn't happen overnight. It took years.

Everything we've built has been a little bit at a time, as we could afford it. Seven Arrows Farm, Attleboro, Massachusetts.

It took many years for us to arrive at a place where our garden accurately represented what we wanted to express. Polygonum aubertii 'Lemon Lace', Perilla frutescens, ceramic sculptures by John Fazzino. The "Tea Garden" at Seven Arrows Farm, Attleboro, Massachusetts.

We used broadleaf evergreens, Prunus lauro-cerassus, and Magnolia grandiflora to create a calming, soothing mood in the "Tea Garden." Seven Arrows Farm, Attleboro, Massachusetts.

Hosta "Chesterland Gold," Pinus thumber-gii, Hosta "Big Daddy" Sculpture, Michel Marcellot. Seven Arrows Farm, Attleboro, Massachusetts.

Clematis heracleifolia, Hakonechloa macra "Albo Striata" Perilla frutascens, Hosta "Chesterland Gold." Seven Arrows Farm, Attleboro, Massachesetts.

Clematis heracleifolia, Hakonechloa macra "Albo Striata", Hosta "Chesterland Gold." Seven Arrows Farm, Attleboro, Massachesetts.

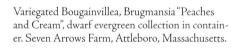

Variegated Bougainvillea, Brugmansia "Peaches and Cream", dwarf evergreen collection in container. Seven Arrows Farm, Attleboro, Massachusetts.

Some achieve enlightenment effortlessly, an example for us all. Seven Arrows Farm, Attleboro, Massachusetts.

Ligularia stenocephala "The Rocket." Seven Arrows Farm, Attleboro, Massachusetts.

Business was steadily improving. We decided to build a new building, a post and beam barn-like structure that would house a store, a tearoom, a classroom, and activity space that would be available to the community at no cost. So we borrowed on the equity of our cozy little New England antique cape (we had put the oil burner back in the house at this point) and hired some young men to help us build our barn. They were a wild and crazy bunch—part-time musicians, followers of the Grateful Dead, and Irish boys who kept us laughing with their dark humor IRA jokes. If the Dead were playing anywhere east of the Mississippi, we would go out in the morning to find just the two Irish boys pounding away. The other carpenters would return when the Dead had recrossed the Mississippi and headed west. Progress was slow, but we spent a lot of time laughing. They taught us how to have fun again. Out with the "nothing but Gregorian chant phase" and in with the "rock and roll!" We were still true to our spiritual journeys but decided we didn't have to be so serious about it.

At one point, the pendulum may have swung a little far over as we found ourselves a bit too involved with "fixing" one of the carpenters who had an alcohol and drug dependency. His addictions manifested in stealing, unreliability, lying, and other common addict behaviors. Our addictions manifested in trying to make everything *all right* for him. He was a wonderfully talented musician whose bread and butter job was carpentry, while he pursued his true joy and passion of singing, songwriting, and studio recording. We thought friendship and exposure to "spiritual people" would heal him (talk about co-dependency!), but it turned out to be the other way around. In this person, we saw the wounded and addict part of ourselves—although our addictions were to other things, like suffering, victim hood, people pleasing at our own emotional expense, and other common so-called co-dependent behaviors. Our year of "Twelve Step" meetings was healing and liberating, and we are grateful for "our addict's" presence in our lives, however painful it may have been at the time. When it became necessary to break off the relationship, we were ready, but had grown in ways we would not have, had we never known one another. And we never think of our days with him without acknowledging how grateful we are for his showing us who we were really were.

We weren't really paying too much attention to the gardens at this time because we were far too busy with the new building and the resulting chaotic energy. The gardens were re-arranging themselves, however. Sun areas became shady, and shade gardens found themselves in full sun.

It became obvious to us that when we created anything, in this case our garden, we were setting in time and space all that we were at that moment. We might have an epiphany seconds later, and choose a diametrically opposite approach, but at each moment of creative activity, we were bringing forth all our beliefs about the reality we were creating in that particular moment. We discovered, at least for us, that the gardens were a very real and accurate picture of our emotional lives, or emotional bodies, as some philosophers call it. This was okay because we came to realize that the garden, as an act of creation, whether hideous or beautiful, was only expressing itself in one time and space. Like a Tibetan sand painting, the moment passes and is finished and blown away. The garden, like us, is in a constant state of change. We can only get it right or wrong for an instant before we move on to the next. We and our gardens are hurtling through space on this magnificent rock we call Earth and change is the only constant. So, if you're frustrated with your garden, or fear it says something unflattering about you, take a deep breath and relax. You'll change. It will change.

It took many years to arrive at the place where our most recent garden project accurately represented what we wanted to express. It took a long time for us to connect with the elements that drew to us what we wanted to see around us. But then, the garden is never done until we're compost, is it?

Things swung back to a comfortable middle ground. More fun, less seriousness, and the same pursuit of the peaceful path. And as we continued to grow and change in our inner world, things changed in the outer. We came to realize that the *pay now collect later* plan was inherently problematic for all the reasons we've already mentioned. And we discovered that suffering, as the Buddhists say, really is optional. It was as simple as choosing not to suffer, always finding a way to make ourselves feel a little better, and then a little bit better, and a little better until, heck, we were downright joyful! Now, we admit, this process could be lengthy. In other words, joy was often not the next logical step in the evolution of how we were feeling. But our lives really began to change when we started to incorporate the not-always-so-simple practice of changing our thoughts, with the objective of changing our feelings, with the objective of changing our outer world. We discovered that how we feel really does determine what we attract and what we manifest.

Gerry and Lea

Gerry would probably describe himself as a college-educated master plumber who returned to plumbing after the company where he worked as a Project Administrator downsized and moved to Texas. Lea worked for many years as a part-time nurse and now designs and paints stained glass in Massachusetts.

"A garden reflects the personality and character of its creators. Ours has evolved along with us over the past thirty-five years, at first an attempt to hide the large excavations attendant to our backfilling efforts and at length a testament to our addiction to managing the Earth and some of its marvelous creations. Our efforts have always been restrained by the budget of a four-child household. Our fervor grew and Lea's Mom and Dad moved next door joining the foray in a big way. We always refer to Ma's garden as the 'Brooklyn Botanic Annex.' Ma never does anything halfway. In 2001, our garden was on the American Hemerocalis Society's annual national tour and featured three hundred or so of some of the world's latest daylily hybrids and a few of our own hybridized daylilies. It was a once-in-a-life time opportunity for ego massage.

Today we're a little less energetic and trying to scale down to reduce garden maintenance. We like to think that 'bigger isn't necessarily better' and refinement is now the way to go. In any case, any garden is by its very nature evolutionary, just by the fact that things grow. And the garden is further influenced directly by the people who manage it and have grown through their own life experiences. Our garden is forever changing, following seasonal rhythms, always begging our participation, always rewarding us with peace, beauty and a profound connection to the Earth, its plants, its creatures. Hybridizing daylilies has taught us that life welcomes our help in the creation of its flowers. The endless surprises of new variations of flowers never fail to delight us. Through the garden we've met new friends, shared walks and conversations, shared its abundance with others, and had moments of gratitude. It's work and fun at the same time.

We are now in the fall season of our lives, and yes, there is still much beauty. Our lives continue to evolve, so we are never quite sure just what is coming next but our garden helps us to accept and celebrate life and change, or what some have called 'impermanence.' It seems that rather than protesting change the Earth encourages it!"

In 2001, Gerry and Lea's garden was selected to be included in the American Hemerocalis Society's national garden tour. Bristol County, Massachusetts.

"Hybridizing daylilies has taught us that life welcomes our help in the creation of its flowers." Some of Gerry and Lea's hybridized daylilies. Bristol County, Massachusetts. *Photos courtesy of Gerry Deschenes*

History, Science and Math for the Folks Who Enjoy It

No matter what tradition or background we come from, or what beliefs we hold, our brains are hard-wired to perceive certain natural phenomena as special, elevating them from the ordinary. They connect us to each other and to the greater cosmos on a level beyond words and worldly concerns. No language is more universal to the human experience than that of the natural realm in both planned and wild form.

Machu Picchu, Peru. In the Quechua language, literally "old peak." People have always been able to sense the power of a place. Recent studies suggest a relationship between geomagnetic earth energies and the location of many sacred sites around the globe, according to Dr. Schoch. *Photo courtesy of Dr. Robert Schoch*

Grand Canyon, Arizona.
Photo courtesy of Remy Omar

Delicate Arch, Arches National Park, Utah. *Photo courtesy of Remy Omar*　　Double Arch, Arches National Park, Utah. *Photo courtesy of Remy Omar*

We perceive our world through the five senses. But we *experience* it emotionally (or vibrationally). Certain sights and images produce emotional responses in us. When we attempt to create peaceful or sanctuary spaces, we're seeking to create images and experiences that evoke feelings that soothe and calm the mind while inspiring the spirit. The bulk of what has been written about gardens is concerned with the visual, how things look to the observer. Here we are principally concerned with how one feels in the garden, how that space makes you *feel* when you occupy it. How you *feel* is everything here!

> *"One of the most important ways that I measure success of a garden is how it changes the way you feel."*
>
> —Holly Shimizu, Executive Director
> U. S. Botanic Garden

Tracing the origin of garden design in his classic book, *A History of Gardens*, Derek Clifford says: *"(One) source of gardens lay in that sense of awe which primitive man felt in certain natural scenery. This is a state of mind for which there is no precise term, but one which most men can still feel especially in circumstances remote from the dulling effect of everyday experience; for example, at night in the bows of a ship, at sunrise on a mountain peak, at dusk in a forest clearing. These sensations of awe led men to worship the genius of the place from which it emanated.*

To such spots men returned again and again, ostensibly to please the Spirit with offerings, but really in order to enjoy the sensation, a sensation akin to fear yet not fear, a sensation dwarfing yet ennobling, not unlike that which a note might feel when included in a symphony. Not only were the more remarkable scenes the homes of great deities, but every small stream became in time the manifestation of a nymph and every tree had a resident dryad. Where this spirit was alive a garden was not only a sanctuary but also a temple for gods." (Clifford, 1963, 23.)

Uluru, sacred to certain Australian aborigines stands out from its surroundings for miles. Unlike other such naturally occurring phenomena, it has not been enhanced architecturally. It's only enhancements are drawings. *Photo courtesy of David Stephenson*

Standing stone circles are found all over the British Isles. Theories abound as to their uses. Were the first landscape architects shamans? Cotswolds, England. *Photo courtesy Alan & Elizabeth Taylor*

Taksang Lhakhang , Tigers Lair Monastery, 10,500 feet above sea level. Paro, Bhutan. Photos courtesy of Brent Olson

Photo courtesy of Remy Omar

"The genius of the place" at Dodona has been recognized by countless societies. The oracle of Zeus at Dodona, Greece, mentioned by Homer, was situated in a sacred grove of oak trees. *Photo courtesy of Carolyn Heathcote*

The archeological record here starts in the eighth century BC, the ruins pictured date to the fourth century BC. The shrine of Dodona was the oldest Hellenic oracle, according to the fifth-century historian Herodotus and in fact dates to pre-Hellenic times, perhaps as early as the second millennium BCE. Priests and priestesses in the sacred grove interpreted the rustling of the oak (or beech) leaves to determine the correct actions to be taken. Contrary to what is often thought, they did not predict the future. This site is very unspoiled and has a very calming atmosphere. *Photo courtesy of Carolyn Heathcote*

Agios Georgios, on Corfu, Greece.
Photo courtesy of Carolyn Heathcote

Here, we are looking at what Clifford calls "the genius of the place." Why do some places feel filled with obvious "genius" and others devoid of it?

Dr. Fred Meli, anthropologist from the University of Rhode Island, puts it this way:

"I think that the affinity with geographic and geological places is as old as the human, or even the proto-hominids. The sacredness of a place was understood to have power, a place where one could sense or even feel the presence of the power, thus, these places were visited and venerated. When humans acquired the ability to reason and see in abstractions they also began to alter, modify and later design effigies and other structures in this veneration and worship. The ancient cave dwellers modeled their later living spaces after the cave, round and with a single entrance."

Clearly the people of Aukland, New Zealand, who erected this frame, consider their unadorned landscape to be a work of art. The inscription on the frame reads, "How to frame a view." *Photo courtesy of Carolyn Heathcote*

The impulse to decorate our surroundings, for whatever reason, seems to be a hardwired activity. Could this be an early indication of human attempts to decorate the landscape? Arches National Park, Utah. *Photo courtesy of Remy Omar*

"*Humans created rituals around these spaces and later built their own spaces, often on the sites of pre-existing geological formations and prominent landscape features such as hills, caves, and rock outcroppings. The earliest of these were megalithic structures and complexes were often dedicated to celestial phenomena that were observable at that location, the Solstice, lunar cycles and other regular celestial events. Often the site had other powers, forces and energy that were discernible. So people returned to the places, and rebuilt them and when there were no longer any remains of the original structure they constructed ones in their stead, to satisfy a need to be connected to the earth. Many humans have lost the ability to sense power in the landscape, thus, they involve themselves with other activities.*

Today humans create landscapes that are pleasing as well as serve a purpose for reflection, and contemplation, such as gardens, and waterfalls, and pools. The act of creating the space is both a meditation and dedication to the veneration of the place, even if they do not understand that is what they are doing."

It was interesting to us that, according to the research of the day, our children's people used principles of geomancy to site both ancestral graves and present day use of land for relaxation and contemplation purposes. This seemed to be true in the home country, Laos, and here in the United States (Elizabeth Sheehan, 1994 "Greens: Hmong Gardens, Farms and Land Ownership in America: Constructing Environment and Identity in the Carolinas", University of Connecticut).

One of the principal objectives in creating a garden for relaxation is to balance and soothe the psyche. We want to create an experience that causes the gardener/visitor to release his or her references to everyday life and let go of the physical effects of the psychological stresses associated with them. We want to redirect the gaze from external to internal. We want to relax. We want to feel at peace.

"I go to nature to be soothed and healed, and to have my senses put in order."

—John Burroughs

> *"These two emotions, joy in relief from stress and hunger for spiritual reawakening, are the remote source of leisured man's garden-making."* (Clifford, 1963, 24.)

Dr. Robert Schoch of Boston University has made his reputation investigating geologic phenomena and their relationship to sacred sites. He has researched sites in Peru, submerged sites off the coast of Japan, and used geologic evidence to push back the construction date of the Sphinx at Giza in Egypt. According to his research, many sites of sacred architecture were built on pre-existing geologic anomalies. He theorizes that the Great Pyramid at Giza was built on a stone formation. Evidence suggests that the tunnel found within it had existed well before the construction of the massive pyramid above.

In addition to the Great Pyramid, the Oracle of Delphi was originally a cave, and later became an architectural masterpiece, the ruins of which still

The Sphinx has been changed several times since the first carving. Using geologic evidence, Dr. Robert Schoch has placed the time of the original carving far before previous estimates. He theorizes that it was venerated before carving began as a natural feature in the landscape even earlier still. *Photo courtesy of Michelle Pitt*

survive as a tourist destination. All over the world, evidence can be found of man's veneration of the landscape in its natural forms. These sites may have undergone artificial enhancement, but the first veneration came as someone, or group of individuals, recognized the spot as special, worthy of note and possessing unique qualities. According to Dr. Schoch, many ancient sacred sites were originally naturally-occurring landscape features. These features were significantly different from the surrounding landscape to have been recognized by ancient-aboriginal man and interpreted as possessing power of an otherworldly nature, *"a temple of the Gods"* as Clifford states.

Over time, these sites were venerated and people started decorating them in the fashion and style of the time, with the technology and materials available to them. Whether ancient-aboriginal humankind possessed some now dormant skill in "feeling" the power of a place, as suggested by Dr. Meli, or these types of landscape features were venerated because they were different from their surroundings, or perceived to be the abode of the Gods, as Clifford suggests, one thing appears to be true: Sanctuary space is created when intention and emotion meet the environment.

It would seem that the impulse to dig in the earth and nurture things that grow is an activity that is hard-wired into the human brain. Whenever we place a spade to earth or stoop to pull a weed, we are joining in an activity that traces its roots back to the dawn of time.

The origins of the mythology of garden as spiritual sanctuary are hard to discern. Some scientists have set the earliest signs of 'civilized' settlements (cities, and recorded histories) at somewhere around 4-5000 BC. Dr. Schoch thinks that early societies, like the hunter-gatherer, had more leisure time than the anthropological community ascribes to them. He cites evidence of 250,000-year-old tools being decorated, clearly more than an activity dedicated to pure survival. If early humans had the time to devote to painting on cave walls and decorating tools, why wouldn't they have seen value in planting or cultivating specific plants that produced a desired result like pleasure? Whatever the time line, it is clear that somewhere back in humankind's history, the impulse to enhance the visual appearance of our surroundings arose in a big way. We took our inspiration from our surroundings.

The Treasury was built by the Athenians at the end of the sixth century BC in order to house their offerings to Apollo. The Oracle of Delphi, dating back to 1400 BC, was the most important shrine in all Greece; people from all over the known world would come to Delphi for advice. In ancient Greece, it was considered the centre of the world.
Photo courtesy of Carolyn Heathcote

Experts say that the human brain develops in three stages in the womb. The first to develop is the ancient "reptilian brain." This is the part that we share with all creatures possessing a brain. It is in control of the basic workings of the body, including involuntary actions, like coronary functions and breathing. The part of the brain which surrounds the archipallium (R-complex reptilian brain) is the "old mammalian" brain. This is where, among other things, the limbic system resides. The limbic system is responsible for behaviors essential to the survival of mammals—nursing the young, the impulse to protect offspring, major emotions like hate, joy, sadness, and the ability to differentiate between like and dislike, for example. In humans, the olfactory bulbs are connected through the limbic system, making it a part of our lower, more primal processes. That's why we can have such instinctive reactions to smells, both pleasant and offensive. It may be somewhere here, in the old mammalian brain, that the first impressions about the outer landscape began to form because this is where fight or flight, hunger, and scent are processed.

Markers in the landscape that are essential to our survival and linked to these raw base instincts are strong and undeniable even in our "modern brain." Who hasn't felt a visceral fear grip them when looking over a cliff or into a dark cave? A sudden clap of thunder or similar loud noise can elicit a similar response, the urge to flee or take cover. These are cues taken from the natural world that produce predictable, instinctual responses. Perhaps seeing things like standing stones, stone circles, water sources and other archetypal geometric symbology produces relatively predictable responses. One only needs to look at the real estate pages to understand the high value placed on water views, mountain views, and scenic vistas. The fact that a higher value is placed on these elements speaks to their desirability. The universality of our response to, and desire for, these scenes is what is noteworthy. The language of water and stones, the ability to see out over the landscape, and the geometry of enclosures elicit a response similar to seeing an old friend in a crowd, recognizability and comfort.

There appears to be a consensus of emotional response to these stimuli, making the enhancement or re-creation of these scenes a logical pursuit for us as we attempt to decorate our living environment. By tapping into the deep origins of these emotional responses, we can see how gardens communicate directly with some deeper part of ourselves, bypassing the rational thinking brain. Ancient temple and public space builders used this knowledge to create spaces that awed and intimidated the populace, as well as their enemies. Architecture was used to great effect to enhance natural landscape features.

There are many common themes found in sacred sites that are simple and universal. There is no reason why we cannot include these in everyday life right now, no matter where we find ourselves. We can begin anywhere. Some of the gardeners whose stories we've collected have created elements—garden mounds, ponds, and streams—meant to resemble natural phenomena. Others have enhanced natural features. Still others have imitated nature in smaller ways. People create spaces that connect them to the Greater Whole, God, Allah, Jehovah, Intelligent Designer, Pure, Positive Energy, (whatever one names that Great Mystery, if it is named at all,) simply by intending it, and having an emotional bond to the space. Or an emotional bond to the process of working the space itself. Aesthetic preferences come and go. Design rules shift. How people feel in their spaces remains the most important factor in creating sanctuary gardens. One of the strongest emotional responses to a garden we experienced during the writing of this book was in a small, city garden dedicated to the memory of its owner's husband. The place practically oozed with the love she felt for her husband and a larger Love at the same time.

Geometry, Yes and No

Geometry is everywhere we look, especially in nature. Initially we saw very simple geometry as a key component of the gardens we most admired and found pleasing, both physically and on an emotional level. Michel was going to call this segment of the book, "It's all about Geometry—you should have listened!" We reasoned that simple designs required the brain to process less information and therefore were more suited to gardens created for rest and reflection. We sought out experts in the fields of quantum physics and fractal geometry to understand better how we perceive our world. However, our initial premise turned out not to be completely correct. It turns out that restfulness is only part of the equation. We also need to be inspired. For inspiration, our brains seek out complexity.

Fractal geometry describes objects that are self-similar. This means that when such objects are magnified, their parts are seen to bear an exact resemblance to the whole, the likeness continuing with the parts of the parts and so on to infinity. It is exciting to scientists because it seems to explain how things grow. Some good examples of this in nature are fern fronds or snowflakes. If you look closely at either, you will find one basic pattern that repeats itself over and over again to make up the whole object. *That's simple*, we thought.

Fractals in Nature

Fortunately, with the help of a friend and landscape client, we were able to find a person who was an expert in math and physics, Dr. Leo Kadanoff, Professor Emeritus of Physics and Math at the University of Chicago. Dr. Kadanoff is widely recognized for his work in statistical physics, chaos theory, and theoretical condensed matter physics. He was nominated for the Nobel Prize in Physics, received the National Medal of Science in the U.S., the Grande Medaille d" Or of the Academy des Sciences de I'Institut de France and many, many other awards and professional recognition. If Dr. Kadanoff couldn't help us understand where geometry fit in, no one could.

We hoped to come up with some generalizations about how we process information in our brains to simplify things, and then describe geometry as the only thing you need to know about how to design a garden. It wasn't that simple, however. We discovered that the mind doesn't just like things simple. There's actually plenty of room for complexity in the human brain.

When we started out as designers, we started with a very nature-informed, natural style, full of curves. We actually avoided straight lines on purpose, having pronounced them boring. Part of this came from learning about plants in the forests, part from current fashion (this was the late 70s), and part just trying to develop a distinctive personal style.

We have been fortunate to meet some amazing people through the business, and one of them is a landscape designer who's client list includes names anyone in America would recognize. We admired his work and gleaned new ideas by examining his projects that relied heavily on simple geometric forms—squares, rectangles and straight lines. We learned that the brain has a "centering" function that causes us to want to move our bodies so we align ourselves with an object or view.

Geometry simplifies things, so we thought, and our brains like simple things, or so we thought. After speaking with Dr Kadanoff, our thinking changed. Dr. Kadanoff told us that the straight line isn't the only interesting shape in the world. The circle has certainly been a shape that has captured people's imagination, but we also get good feeling from clouds. The richness of these structures impresses us, he told us. He went on to tell us that his colleagues who work on vision, contend that our vision is designed to enable us to take in very complicated things and perhaps make some sense out of them.

> *"When I look in the garden I don't see only simple circles. I see things that are vastly richer and I have to make sense of them. The shapes 'circle' and 'square' help us describe natural things around us, and the words 'again and again and again' also help our mind mathematically define natural things around us. Many, many rivulets combine naturally to create streams, and many streams combine to form the huge Mississippi river that flows into the ocean. This is a natural process. The same process occurs in nature repeatedly. A tree divides into branches over and over again, the roots branch out again and again, and trees produce leaves over and over again."*
>
> —Dr. Leo Kadanoff, June, 2006

Fern fronds are made of thousands of leaflets, each the same, repeated over again and again. *Photo courtesy of Rodd Halstead Photography*

Photo courtesy of Ian Wright

Photo courtesy of Jean Simard

Geometry is everywhere you look. Nature has organized itself geometrically since the beginning. Here we see an image generated by feeding a formula into a computer. Many "fractal generators" can be found on the internet. From ferns, snowflakes, and trees to complete river systems, it's amazing to see how many naturally occurring phenomena can be generated this way. Math can be beautiful! *Image courtesy of Rodd Halstead Photography*

Zingiber spectabile, Beehive Ginger at the Chelsea Garden Show, London England. *Photo courtesy of Carolyn Heathcote*

Echinops ritro, Lamoille County, Vermont.
Photo courtesy of Paul Moody

Photo courtesy of Irena Suchocki

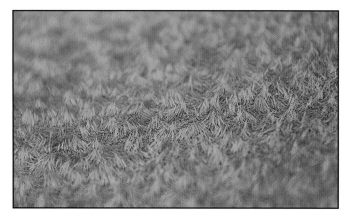

Hairy frost, Lamoille County, Vermont. *Photo courtesy of Paul Moody*

Rosa species. *Photo courtesy of Irena Suchocki*

Photo courtesy of Lenny Zimmerman

Our brains have a "centering" function which causes us to want to move our bodies in order to place line ourselves up to center a view. Palace of Versailles outside Paris, France. *Photo courtesy of Anna Rosinska*

Bricks are all the same size rectangle, yet the impression is of circles and arches. A pattern repeated again and again takes on a life of its own. Brick work by Seven Arrows Farm. Location: Providence County, Rhode Island.

Look at any public space, a park or public garden, and you'll see very simple squares, rectangles and circles. This is calming to the brain because there is little complexity to process. While it may be calming, our brains may want more, however. Complexity is important too, according to Dr. Kadanoff. We look for richness as well. There's a place for both simplicity and complexity in the garden.

Too much complexity isn't calming. Too much simplicity isn't inspiring.

"Mathematics and beauty have interacted in many different ways. Renaissance paintings were formed by issues of perspective which were essentially mathematical and geometrical in character."— Dr. Leo Kadanoff. Could it be the combination of simple and complex geometry is what makes this view from the top of the Eiffel Tower in Paris, France appealing? We all react to different proportions of order to disorder in similar ways. Some favor a higher concentration of one over the other, but it is the combination of the two that is interesting to us. Paris, France. *Photo courtesy of Stella McLoughlin*

"We certainly leave behind our thoughts in terms of the artistic and architectural objects we create. They represent our thoughts and emotions. We leave them behind for future generations to understand and interpret. This is true of gardens and parks, too".

—Dr. Leo Kadanoff

"I've made an odd discovery. Every time I talk to a savant I feel quite sure that happiness is no longer a possibility. Yet when I talk with my gardener, I'm convinced of the opposite."

—Bertrand Russell

Desire is Good

We spent many long years working through the "desire" issue. Being on a spiritual journey throughout our lives, and particularly our lives together, brought us in contact with belief systems and philosophies that held the act of desire as something to be "worked through," "put a ceiling on," "overcome," "let go of," etc. It wasn't until we made peace with the whole energy surrounding desire, and judged it as not only very acceptable, but impossible to live without, that our lives really started to manifest, as we desired them, not as we wished them. We started to see desire as the source of creation, rather than an impediment to it. How could we plant a garden without the desire to experience what the garden offered? How could we renovate our house without the desire to live in a more beautiful, comfortable place? How can we do anything creative without the desire that funds motivation and creativity? Human beings are born with desire. Why would we want to deny such a huge part of ourselves? Desire became our friend and we felt like we had won the lottery! Lots of "new thought" philosophers speak of desire as being the first step in creating and living deliberate lives of joy, abundance, peace, etc. Humans seem to do this automatically, sending out "rockets of desire" all the time. Desire in this context is neither positive nor negative, simply a building block of creating. It works for us, as gardeners and as human beings!

Desire for sanctuary is fundamental to our mental health. We want to feel safe, to feel secure in our homes and in the space surrounding our homes. Sanctuary is essentially a feeling or place we go in our emotional bodies. Gardens, which contain elements or symbols meaningful or significant to the viewer, can uplift, inspire and move the mind into a calm state. While there are universal elements that promote this (rock, water, aroma), it is the individual who is the ultimate decider of what makes him or her feel peaceful, relaxed, nurtured, etc. Peaceful experiences draw more peaceful experiences, contentment more contentment, and on and on in a universe that is attraction based. *Like* really does attract *like*.

Valerianna—Teacher, Healer, Artist

"After twelve years living in the city, I longed for a country home with land that I could steward and that I felt I belonged to. Searching the internet for land in Western Massachusetts became a daily ritual as did sitting with a candle and calling on the spirit of my new home to find me. One day a house popped up on my computer screen and shivers went up my spine. This was my home. On my first visit to what would become my sanctuary, I took a walk into the forest after seeing the house. Snowy patches stuck to rock ledges and the hemlock branches danced in the breeze. I stopped just a short distance into the woods, struck by the intensity of the green ferns and mosses peering out from under the snow and the depth of silence. Offering prayer in the form of a song, I stopped, suddenly breathless, tears running down my face. This was home; this was where I belonged, where the land speaks to me, where I melt into the sacred.

Three years later, gardens have taken root in the clearing around the house, sculptures find homes on top of moss covered tree stumps and stacks of stone mark pathways and provide lookouts for the resident chipmunks. When I walk to the edge of the forest, I feel that I am standing at the threshold to another realm, and entering, I sense the spirit that called me here to remember the wild nature within myself. She shows up as the Barred Owl sitting on the tree next to the house, napping in the sunshine as I stack wood, and as the bear that trundles off catching us both by surprise when we meet on the path."

Hampshire County, Massachusetts.
Photo Courtesy of Valerianna Claff

Hampshire County, Massachusetts.
Photo Courtesy of Valerianna Claff

*"When I walk to the edge of the forest, I feel that I
am standing at the threshold to another realm, and
entering…"* Hampshire County, Massachusetts.
Photo Courtesy of Valerianna Claff

Hampshire County, Massachusetts. *Photo Courtesy of Valerianna Claff*

Hampshire County, Massachusetts. *Photo Courtesy of Valerianna Claff*

Hampshire County, Massachusetts.
Photo Courtesy of Valerianna Claff

Hampshire County, Massachusetts. *Photo Courtesy of Valerianna Claff*

Intention is Everything

There has been a lot said and written these days about holding clear intent, focusing, and setting your compass in a clear direction. Intention, some folks believe, is everything. We would hold that if intention isn't everything, it's a big part of the grand picture. When we set out to create our little nursery, for example, we listed our ideals—larger categories of a more generalized nature under which would fall the specifics of what we wanted to create. That the universe responded to our thoughts and feelings wasn't a new idea even at that time, nearly thirty years ago, but an important one for us. Today, this way of thinking is quite accepted in the philosophical and metaphysical communities. Books and movies speaking to this are out there in the mainstream media. Although we really didn't have a clear vision of what we wanted the nursery and gardens to look like, we had very clear ideas about what we wanted them to *feel* like. We wanted to feel, well basically, peaceful when we were in them. And we wanted others to feel at peace here, as well. We were familiar with different processes for setting ideals on the esoteric, feeling, and physical levels. We were clear about the (higher) ideals, but left the details and minutiae to an ever-expanding universe.

In the physical, this resulted in our largest space morphing from a horse pasture to a raised bed garden of sun loving herbs, to a perennial shade garden when the Bradford pear tree grew from a five-foot sapling to its twenty-foot maturity. Then, after a series of windstorms and hurricanes, the garden returned to its original sunny state when the pear finally came down. Bradford pears are lovely and are often used as street trees here in New England, but as fast-growing soft wood trees, they do not have a very long life span—twenty years or so. Now that space has a European feel to it—a classic walled space surrounding a crushed stone patio with plantings chosen to subtly change in form and foliage, but not sharply contrasting to one another. To this end, we have planted Cherry laurels, Upright yews, Witch hazel, Hydrangea paniculata and Magnolia grandiflora. At any rate, we are happy with the space the way it is now, but we can see it changing still—painting the wall, adding some lush tropicals that will need to be brought in for the winter, and adding another table for sitting. It takes us a long time to plant a new space, as the two of us need to agree, and sometimes it takes a long time for that to happen. Everything, the garden included, unfolds in its own time.

When we built the post and beam building (which houses our store, four season tea room, loft space for community activities like weddings, classes, small theatrical productions, barn dances and community sings, etc.), we wrote our "larger" intention in the concrete foundation of the building before it hardened:

"To manifest the Love of God in the Earth through Peace, Joy and Freedom."

While we might phrase it differently now—we've grown and changed after all—we are not unhappy with the original choice. We wanted to create a space where people could come, sit, relax, enjoy the sights and scents of each season, and feel connected to something larger. It didn't matter to us how one named that Great Presence or if one named it at all. It was important that our intention be clear, at least to us. Judging from comments of visitors to our gardens and nursery, over the years, our initial intent is obvious to lots of people

> "I shut my eyes in order to see."
> —Paul Gauguin

Jan—Artist

"Intentions? The word seems to convey what I am doing when I work on the slates as well as what I hope the people who purchase them feel when they add them to their space or give them to someone else. I have been making an effort to incorporate mindful living into my daily actions for the past few years. My art project has been a wonderful lesson in that effort. It has been both a gift and a challenge. I feel as though I have been an observer of this process that has allowed me not to be critical or expectant of the results. Washing the slates and honoring what and where they have been for many years gives me a sense of inter-being with all of that. Testing and playing with brushes, strokes, paints, inks and the wonderful literature on Chinese writing and symbols has been both meditative and opening for me.

My hope, as an artist, is that by offering these works I am offering a buyer a reminder to participate in these experiences (mindfulness, openness, and interconnection with All Life). I've had passers-by comment on them hanging on my fence. One fellow came in and took pictures. What an opportunity to connect in a peaceful way with strangers! I think of them as gentle reminders to reconnect with our Buddha nature. "

Intention Plaques. by Jan Hindley

Jan.

Elementals, Fairies, Gnomes, and the Others

"Enter" Kingsmere Estate, Gatineau Park, Quebec Canada. *Photo courtesy of Irene Suchocki*

When we began our plant nursery, a woman who claimed to talk to these other dimensional creatures would visit regularly, play her recorder in one of the greenhouses and have animated and lively conversations with different fairies, gnomes, and the like. In writing this book, we have encountered very respectable members of the community who fully accept the existence of this realm of consciousness. Not long ago, we ran into a friend at the market, a well-respected British-born musician. We began talking about what part of this book we were working on and he said, in all seriousness, *"Not all of them are nice, you know. I have a mean little bunch living in my basement."* We've actually not run across any groups of mean elementals ourselves, but we've learned to accept everyone's reality as they describe it. This makes life more fun than second-guessing and judging, we think.

People generally line up on classifying elementals—gnomes, fairies, elves, etc.—as either existing as folklore and fairy tales, being real in some other dimension or consciousness, or they are simply unsure of whether they're real or not. Different cultures have different names for these beings, which have included gnomes, elves, fairies, nature spirits, elementals, angels, and on and on. Countries all over the globe have a place for this in their folklore. There are hundreds of names for these beings—devs (Persian), yowahoos (African), shedim (Jewish), afries (Egyptian) to name a few.

William Bloom's little book, *Devas. Fairies and Angels. A Modern Approach* states:

> *"Throughout history, in all cultures, in all major religions and in all geographical areas, men and women have talked and written about beings and creatures who belong to another magical, religious or psychic dimension. These creatures are not human beings in another dimension, but are a distinct and different life form. They manifest themselves in a wondrous variety—from the tiny fairies who sleep in the buds of buttercups through to awesome Archangels who wield cosmic force itself."* (Bloom, 1986, 1.)

Always believe in the faeries. *Photo courtesy of Melissa Tanner*

Quebec, Canada. *Photo courtesy of Irene Suchocki*

Photo courtesy of Irene Suchocki

Photo courtesy of Irene Suchocki

Bloom asks,

"Well, what are we to make of all this? There seem to be three possibilities: The first is that for thousands of years storytellers, in folklore and religious text, have enjoyed simply inventing these beings. The second possibility is that the human brain and human psyche are structured in such a way that regardless of time, culture or geography, people always imagine and hallucinate in the same form. The third possibility is that devas are indeed a reality, but that they exist in a dimension normally not perceivable by the usual five human senses, and therefore, incapable of being proven by contemporary science." (Bloom, 1986, 1.)

We remember a lovely afternoon we spent many years ago visiting friends in the seaside town of Marblehead, Massachusetts. The couple had authored several booklets of spiritual guidance, quotes, and inspirational stories. They mentioned in passing that there was a very nice tree spirit named Nathan on our property. We guessed that it must be the handsome scrub oak behind the building housing our store. We've addressed the tree as Nathan every since. Here is how he looks today.

Photo courtesy of Irene Suchocki

Not long ago we ran across a Reuters piece by one Rolf Soderlind titled, "Elves in Modern Iceland," which provided a good laugh with our morning tea. Mr. Soderlind wrote of the problems which began when construction equipment started mysteriously breaking down on a road building project outside of Reykjavik, the capitol of Iceland. Work ground to a complete halt, in fact, in front of one particular stone. The problem was approached in rather a unique fashion, Icelanders being open to the existence of elves, fairies, and gnomes, etc. A medium was called in to see if fairy folk were behind any, or all, of the shenanigans.

"Our basic approach is not to deny this phenomenon," an engineer with the Iceland Road Authority, told Reuters. *"We tread carefully. There are people who can negotiate with the elves, and we make use of that."*

The medium reported that the elves told her, while they no longer lived in the stone, they wanted their former residence treated respectfully, and not just blown to smithereens. According to one journalist, elves found themselves being interviewed (although indirectly) for what is believed to be a historical first. According to the story, construction continued without further problems after the dignified removal of the rock.

Internationally published author and visionary artist, Sasha St. John, wrote of her long time connection to the elemental realm.

"Years ago, under hypnosis, I described wild visions of the faeries. The entities that I saw were exceedingly diverse. That experience impacted me greatly as I realized that what I perceive as faery, devas, nature angels, or nature spirits could be very different from someone else's experience. Now I ask all kinds of people about their faery beliefs. Some people see them as a fantasy or a children's tale, and some are not sure what to believe, but very often they say they hope that faeries are real. A surprising number of people say without doubt that faeries exist and they have had experiences with them. Many people I speak with about faery energy confide to me that because their eyes do not perceive a visual form of a faery they discount what they experience. This is understandable for faeries are considered fantasy in many cultures. This can make it challenging for people to share their perceptions of these subtle energies or to stand up and say they experience faeries."

Coleus, Petunia hybrida. Worcester County, Massachusetts.

Worcester County, Massachusetts.

As we write, science has already mathematically proven the existence of a number of dimensions beyond the perceived three or four, if you count passage of time. So we shall see what interesting "new" concepts science reveals to us. In the meantime, pick one of Bloom's possibilities and believe what feels comfortable. Have fun creating fairy circles, fairy gardens, fairy houses. Celebrate Midsummer Night's Eve, which Shakespeare thought to be a night of magic and fairy shenanigans, or connect some other way as some of these gardeners have done, if you like. Believe what you will. There are probably as many ways to perceive reality, as there are perceivers of reality. We found great joy in connecting with these gardeners, their stories, and the part of ourselves that are open to the phenomena of the unseen.

> *"Every square inch of this planet is an amazing miracle. We are surrounded by entities and energies that can support, surprise, delight, teach, and comfort. It is so beautiful! For me, one of the benefits of embracing faery energy is that it reminds me that everything is sacred and that I'm surrounded by beauty, magic and support."*
>
> —Sasha St. John

Linda - Social Worker

"I will tell you a story about myself and my garden and how I was visited by someone who I called a creature of Mother Earth and nature, who came and shared with me. It's what I needed and wanted at that time. My garden means everything to me. My garden is my expression of myself, my inner self, my love of nature, my appreciation of the Goddess and Mother Earth who I love. It's also a form of creative expression. It's very important for me to have that outlet. It is also therapy to me because I have a difficult job at times and my job can create stress and worry for me about the people I serve. I need a way to release the stress in a way that's healthy for me. So I use my garden in all those ways. What attracts me about the garden are the form and the colors—I'm drawn to purples. I'm drawn to pinks. I'm drawn to silver. I'm drawn to lamb's ears and lavender. I have to have purple. Purple means something to me in the garden. It makes me feel good. I have irises of all types. I have baptisia. I have salvia. Oh, there are so many. All my hostas have pink-purple flowers. I have many, many hostas. I love hostas. They make me happy. Something about their shape and their leaves and their variety. During the winter, when I don't get to go out and wander in my garden, I feel a loss. I feel a void in my life until I'm finally able to go out again. I do go out in winter but it's not the same. If I did not have my garden, I don't know what I would do.

A year ago, I was working in my garden. I had taken the day off because I was having a rough time. I started pulling weeds and puttering about, touching and talking to my plants. After an hour or two, I said to myself, 'I wish I had somebody who could come and share this beautiful garden with me.' Right after I said that a beautiful chickadee came and sat on my sunflower so close I could have touched it. But I didn't. I just looked. I said, 'Thank you for coming and sharing my garden with me.' That chickadee sat there for over an hour. It chirped and it moved around a little bit. I just puttered around. I was feeling very good and, after awhile, the bird chirped a little more and flew away. I think Mother Earth knew my need and sent one of its little guardians to help me through.

At the bottom of my stonewall there are little spaces, like doorways. I think that fairies might live there. Something lives there. When I walk by I say, 'Hi. How're you doing today?' I've been thinking about fairies since I was a kid. I still have the books my mother bought for me as a child. I remember going into the backyard, by myself, and reading. I believe in fairies, in Mother Nature showing herself to us in many ways. I also believe fairies are attracted to places where they're accepted, where they're appreciated, valued, understood. People who do not understand or are not open-minded may never see them. Maybe they're afraid. Maybe they don't want to see them. But I search for them. I'm open to them. So I think that's why there are fairies in my garden and in the woods."

Linda with grandson. Worcester County, Massachusetts.

Rudbeckia "Goldstrum." Worcester County, Massachusetts.

Sedum "Frosty Morn." Worcester County, Massachusetts.

Stachys byzantina, Chelone oblique, Veronica "Crater Lake Blue." Worcester County, Massachusetts.

Rudbeckia "Goldstrum." Worcester County, Massachusetts.

Worcester County, Massachusetts.

Hakonachloa macra "Aureola." Worcester County, Massachusetts.

Worcester County, Massachusetts.

Worcester County,
Massachusetts.

We haven't asked
Maggie if she sees the
faeries. We assume
she does. Worcester
County, Massachu-
setts.

Worcester County, Massachusetts.

Worcester County, Massachusetts.

Worcester County, Massachusetts.

Jenna—Singer/Songwriter.

"I am a singer-songwriter and I write in the Celtic style. My songs are deeply influenced by gardens and the working fields, which were considered holy places by the ancient Celts. I have always had a fascination with Celtic legends, not only because it's part of my family heritage but also because their simple concepts of balance and oneness can benefit us today. The Celts had a deep connectedness to Nature. They believed that each tree, plant, animal, even each stone had a spirit. Fairy lore is a part of Celtic tradition. The Fairies were considered the guardians of nature, not the Tinkerbelle pixies we think of today. Fairies connect our world to the Otherworld, the spirit world. The Otherworld was so close at hand that at 'magic times'—dawn, dusk, solstice, etc.—a human being could unwittingly slip through the misty veils and end up in this spirit realm. Often this person would receive important messages, gifts or inspiration before returning to the human realm.

I often go out into my garden to write my songs. I ask the fairies for inspiration. Fairy lore says that being in the presence of fairies can sometimes warp a human's sense of time. I will sit down with my pen and paper and suddenly there's a song in my handwriting on the page. The inspiration comes like such a whirlwind that I feel I must have slipped through those misty veils."

Some people become frightened or threatened by others who talk openly about their perceptions of reality, which may differ dramatically from accepted or popular belief systems. Or they judge the beliefs of others as nonsensical, crazier, something less then their own beliefs. In the spiritual world there are probably as many belief systems as there are believers, although people tend to come together in groups of more or less commonality of belief, holding some tenets as true, others not, or maybe partly so. Some of us go on our merry way, trying to listen to our inner beings, staying connected to pure, positive energy and feelings of joy and dancing the dance of life! Lucky us, we get to choose!

Providence County, Rhode Island. *Photo courtesy of Doug Greene*

Of Frogs and Animals

People have been placing objects that hold personal meaning for them in their gardens and landscapes forever. All kinds of things, from the natural to manmade, add color, texture, and beauty, and can stimulate feelings of peace, joy, contentment, and tranquility. Objects, obviously, can also elicit other reactions. Who hasn't looked at a sculpture or installation and thought, "What the heck were they thinking?" Garden accessories can make you laugh as well. A good laugh is always a great thing.

Several years ago, a concrete frog went missing from a nearby town. A month or so later, the owners started receiving pictures of their frog in front of Buckingham Palace, the Eiffel tower, the Vatican, riding in a gondola through the canals of Venice, and on and on. They shared their photos with the local news station and it was great fun to see what Froggy was up to. A year or so passed and they received a message from the frog's kidnappers saying Froggy was returning home. Sure enough, the frog showed up in a chauffeur driven limousine with a bottle of champagne, as we recall. Apparently, Froggy had a wonderful time, but is happy to be home and bolted down safely in the yard! It still makes us laugh when we see a concrete statue of a frog sitting on a bench. We've since discovered that this kind of kidnapping goes on regularly, especially with gnomes and pink flamingos.

Frogs hold special places in the folklore and symbolic life of many cultures. They have been viewed as divine benevolent symbols of rebirth, transformation, and healing by the Olmecs and other tribes of the Americas. Frogs and toads shed their skins, at least once and usually often during their lifetimes, for example. The Egyptians worshipped a goddess named Heqet, whose head was that of a frog. Heqet was revered as the Goddess of Childbirth and Rebirth. Her priestesses were probably trained as midwives.

Frogs and toads have also been not so positive providers of fortune. The overpopulation of frogs, the second of the plagues visited upon Egypt in the Old Testament book of Exodus, could hardly have been seen as a welcome divine intervention. In medieval Europe, they were symbols of both dark and light magic. Spells were cast, deadly potions concocted, all using frogs and toads. Fairy tale princes were probably not delighted to find themselves turned into frogs by wicked sorcerers.

Yet, gardeners love their frogs. One of our friends dug a pond, when she was very large with child, for the sole purpose of attracting frogs to the yard. Frogs, living or in statue form, hold special meanings for many gardeners as well. We love frogs, too. Our man-made ponds actually attract many frogs and we spend a lot of time rescuing them from one or another of our many beloved cats.

Where's the real froggy? Bristol County Massachusetts.

Frogs hold special places in the folklore and symbolic life of many cultures. Bristol County, Massachusetts.

Bristol County, Massachusetts.

Our man-made ponds attract many frogs, and we spend a lot of time rescuing them from the cats. Bristol County, Massachusetts.

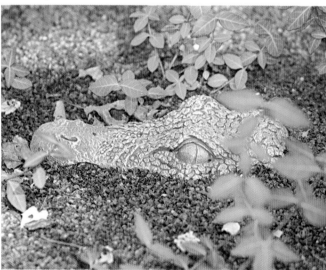

Pinhole photograph. *Courtesy of Sheila Bocchine*

Sue and Steve—Substitute Teacher, Communications

Over the years, two of our neighbors and longtime customers at our nursery would often share pictures of their frogs. According to them, frogs did not naturally populate their two man-made ponds. Each year in early spring, Sue would have to shop for tadpoles in local pet shops. They would watch them grow into frogs. Some would stay for a few years, but more often, the adult frogs would leave during a heavy rain to find a mate, they guessed. One year, Steve noticed a small green frog swimming in the pool of some friends. Knowing that chlorine will kill frogs, Steve caught it, drove home and let it go in the pond. One month later, the frog had doubled in size.

"No wonder," says Sue. *"Every night Steve feeds his frogs night crawlers from the local bait shop. The teeny tiny rescued frog waits for worms to 'fall from the sky' each morning. We've recently made a few trips to catch some tadpoles at a pond in the neighborhood. We enjoy watching them go through their stages of growth. At this same pond, we captured ten baby toads. They were smaller than a pencil eraser. We let them go in an area that is full of hostas and other shade loving plants. We hope that they make it to adulthood and decide to live in our small but 'toadally' creature friendly yard!"*

Mom, is that you? Ontario, Canada. *Photo courtesy of Darlene Greydanus*

And Other Inanimate Objects

Detail of "Dread Christ."
Photo courtesy of Jonny Baker

"Dread Christ" created by Joel Baker. Ealing, England.

Cambria City, California. *Photo courtesy of Javier Esteban Sepulveda*

Cambria City, California. *Photo courtesy of Javier Esteban Sepulveda*

Cambria City, California.
*Photo courtesy of Javier
Esteban Sepulveda*

Bristol County, Massachusetts. *Photo courtesy of Tim Valentine*

Hecate. Otrora, Chile. *Photo courtesy of Yolanda Molina*

Rownton Castle. Shropshire, England. *Photo courtesy of Rob Corbett*

Seven Arrows Farm. Attleboro, Massachusetts.

Even silent, the chimes can provide calm as a place to rest the eyes. Lamoille County, Vermont. *Photo courtesy of Paul Moody*

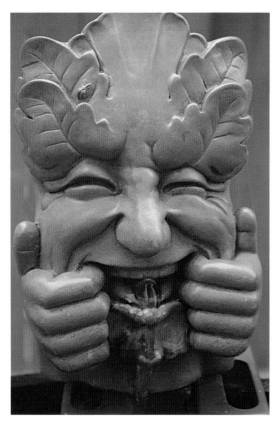

The Green Man can be traced to many different cultures. He is a symbol of resurrection and renewed spirit. Providence County, Rhode Island.

Providence County, Rhode Island.

Providence County, Rhode Island.

The cross symbol predates Christianity by several centuries, first appearing as the junction of two paths. Bristol County, Massachusetts.

The photographer says: *"We always admire these controlled chaos gardens as do the butterflies and songbirds. We have often seen the owners out enjoying a cup of tea and thought to ourselves how peaceful it will be when we can have our own little peace sanctuary for private tea parties like this one."* Mystic, Connecticut. *Photo courtesy of Eric Heupel*

"I bought this chair for $5.00 while out on a country drive. I had hoped that it would be the object of a still life painting, a new venture in my life. But instead, it found its way into the garden. I'm also developing a Mary garden and a labyrinth." Paris, Ontario, Canada. *Photo courtesy of Fleur-Ange Lamothe*

While traditionally viewed as protection from malevolent spirits, some theorize that grotesque images act to lend contrast to beauty. *Photo courtesy of Chanda Star DiMartini*

Garden gargoyle. Surrey, England.
Photo courtesy of Wendy Purdy

"To attract good fortune, spend a new coin on an old friend, share an old pleasure with a new friend, and lift up the heart of a true friend by writing his name on the wings of a dragon." Chinese Proverb. Belfast, Northern Ireland *Photo courtesy of Mel Cameron Radford*

Angels, Saints, and Of Course, the Buddha

Florence, Italy. *Photo courtesy of Giorgio Castelini*

St. Mary, outside the author's home town. Grenoble, France. *Photo courtesy of Jacques Bauer*

La Virgin de Guadalupe. San Antonio, Texas. *Photo courtesy of Bill Norris*

Mary in the garden. Brooklyn, New York. *Photo courtesy of Anne Bowerman*

"All things appear and disappear because of the concurrence of causes and conditions. Nothing ever exists entirely alone; everything is in relation to everything else."

—Buddha

Photo courtesy of Paul Moody

Photo courtesy of Paul Moody

Photo courtesy of Chanda StarDiMartini

"As irrigators lead water where they want, as archers make their arrows straight, as carpenters carve wood, the wise shape their minds." —Buddha. *Photo courtesy of Chanda Star DiMartini*

Photo courtesy of John Suler

Statues of St. Francis rank high with us. St. Francis is well known for his compassion for animals but, in fact, all nature mirrored the divine to him. His compassion was for the entire ecology and in another time and space who knows, we might have been drawn to lives as Franciscan monks. We have reproductions of medieval icons of St. Francis hanging in our home and Judy wears St. Francis medals that friends have brought back from their visits to Assisi, Italy. So, it's only natural that we have what we consider a lovely St. Francis statue in one our shade gardens that we have used in separate exhibition gardens at both the Rhode Island and New England flower shows. Over the years, we have noticed many, many other non-Catholic gardeners like ourselves looking for statues of St. Francis as well.

We used to have a lovely statue of St. Fiacre, but he succumbed to too many New England winters. St. Fiacre is considered to be the patron saint of gardeners (and cab drivers) due to a story involving the cultivation of a garden. Born in Ireland in the seventh century, Fiacre journeyed to France when the devotion of his followers disturbed the peace and isolation he sought. His veneration as saint, and later appearance as a garden statue, came about after he established himself in Meaux and went to the local bishop to ask for land upon which to plant food and herbs. St. Faro, then bishop, reputedly gave Fiacre as much land as he could cultivate in a day. According to legend, trees fell, bushes uprooted, and the ground was cultivated wherever Fiacre touched the earth with his spade. Some locals called it sorcery, but the bishop declared it a miracle, hence Fiacre's future veneration as the Patron Saint of Gardeners.

St. Francis. Portland, Oregon. *Photo courtesy of Rick Wheelock*

Houston, Texas. *Photo courtesy of Jim Evans*

County Wicklow, Ireland. *Photo courtesy of Desmond Cannon (A.K.A Steiner62)*

Pan is always welcoming in the garden. Melbourne, Australia. *Photo courtesy of Katie Tarpey*

"I purchased this angel following the death of my husband. He was English and the one who did most of the gardening. I have taken up the gardening now, gardening with the grandchildren. My husband's grandchildren won't remember him, but I hope to pass on his love of gardening." Paris, Ontario, Canada. *Photo courtesy of M. Fleur-Ange Lamothe*

Labyrinths

In the early 1990s, a friend suggested we build a labyrinth. There weren't many home models in those days, and not a heck of a lot of information on how to make one, although people were just starting to write about the interesting aspects of "walking the labyrinth"—peace, personal growth, etc. Our friend, Terry, kept coming by saying, *"You know, we should do a labyrinth."* We found a basic how-to video by a dowser from Vermont and off we went. It was not a fancy labyrinth. Terry cut a seven-circle pattern into the grass in the back field and we let wild grasses and flowers grow up to form an edging of sorts. We loved it. Many people came to walk it. One beautiful summer's evening, we walked out to the field to discover a group of nuns quietly walking to a beautiful tape-recorded piece of music, candles in hand. It was a magnificently perfect moment. One day, the developer, who we had challenged for so many years in hearings and commissions and court, won permission to build thirty plus houses within a few hundred feet of the labyrinth. To every thing there is a season, and it seemed like it was time for the labyrinth to go. We miss our labyrinth but will build one again some day.

Ealing, England. *Photo courtesy of Jonny Baker*

It's amazing what you can do with a lawnmower and some string. Ealing, England. *Photo courtesy of Jonny Baker*

Labyrinths can be made with a variety of materials. Ealing, England. *Photo courtesy of Jonny Baker*

Stone

Stones of all shapes and sizes have been venerated by diverse cultures from the most ancient of times. Humans love stones. We have arranged large stones in patterns, stood them on edge, and organized them into massive pyramidal structures. Stones, whether displayed individually, or arranged in groups, aligned to celestial events like solstice and equinox, or seemingly random stones in open fields, speak to humans in an archetypal language, penetrating deep into the psyche. We love the odd shaped stone, the smooth stone you can slip into a pocket or skip across a body of water.

Lamoille County, Vermont. *Photo courtesy of Paul Moody*

"The block of granite which was an obstacle in the pathway of the weak becomes a stepping-stone in the pathway of the strong." —Thomas Carlyle, 1795-1881. Stone is our favorite material to work with. Private residence. Providence County, Rhode Island.

*"Rock balancing is a kind of contemplation/meditation for me and to photograph is my deepest passion so all the rock balancing pictures are called ~soulplay~."*Sculptures by Sandra Serretti. Sihltal, Switzerland. *Photo courtesy of Sandra Serretti*

"The pebble in the brook secretly thinks itself a precious stone." Japanese proverb. Sculptures by Sandra Serretti. Sihltal, Switzerland
Photo courtesy of Sandra Serretti

"Those who contemplate the beauty of the earth find reserves of strength that will endure as long as life lasts. There is something infinitely healing in the repeated refrains of nature—the assurance that dawn comes after night, and spring after winter." —Rachel Carson. Staffordshire, England. Photo courtesy of Alan & Elizabeth Taylor

Biddulph Grange, Staffordshire England. *Photo courtesy of Alan & Elizabeth Taylor*

Sculpture, Michel Marcellot. Private residence. Providence County, Rhode Island.

Sculpture, Michel Marcellot. Private residence. Providence County, Rhode Island.

"Give all to love; obey thy heart."
—Ralph Waldo Emerson. Lamoille County, Vermont. *Photo courtesy of Paul Moody*

Although this appears to be an ancient standing stone formation, it is actually an installation of artist Manolo Paz in 1995. Called "Bosque de Menhires," it draws from the ancient, enduring form of the obelisk or standing stone. It is easy to see the power of this form and understand why it has endured so long. Galicia, Spain. *Photo courtesy of Raphael Fernandez Leiro*

In Chinese garden theory, stone occupies a central role as the bones and architecture of the garden. From ancient times, Chinese texts reveal an intense reverence for stone, and the mountains they form. More important, however, is the place stone occupies in the metaphysical and philosophic structure of the garden. The Chinese garden designer looks for stone to reflect and appear "like" the surrounding landscape, or an animal, mythical or real. Rocks can appear, with a little help from the imagination, to be mountain ranges, valleys, and distant forests. This helps transport the visitor to the garden into another miniature world, offering the visitor a sense of unique perspective over the landscape. This disorientation is intentional and serves to unhinge the mind from its terrestrial, everyday view, helping to suspend the garden visitor's grasp of time. In other words, helping the viewer to be in the moment, to "be here now."

Frank Lloyd Wright spoke about people's need for both perch and nest in designing living spaces. While not everybody can live on a mountaintop, arranging rocks in a manner imitating this perspective can satisfy our need for a perch.

Stones, placed upright in the landscape, have appeared throughout the ages.

So, what is it human beings find so special about stone, apart from it being the skeleton of a garden, giving focus and structure year round? Why do so many people speak of the palpable feeling present in ancient temples, mosques, and cathedrals? Judy remembers, as a teenager in England, living across the lane from a tiny village church built of stone in the 1300s. She would spend hours sitting in the damp, unheated building because "it felt so good." Many esoteric philosophies believe stone holds vibration, that is, that stone holds intention.

Stone is often referred to as a heat sink, absorbing heat radiation from the sun and warm air to release it at night when the temperature falls. Hundreds of years of intentions, hopes, and prayers have soaked into the stonewalls of these little country churches and massive cathedrals and mosques alike. Like the heat of a summer day, they emit back the energy put into them from these activities. Stone in the garden does the same thing for all of us.

Bristol County, Massachusetts.

Stone itself is often viewed as timeless. "Diamonds are forever." The phrase "cast in stone" reflects the collective consensus of something lasting and immovable.

A garden built for a geologist. When asked what types of stone he preferred in his garden, he replied:

"There are no bad rocks."

Bristol County, Massachusetts.

Bristol County, Massachusetts.

Bristol County, Massachusetts.

Bristol County, Massachusetts.

"As a rock on the seashore he standeth firm, and the dashing of the waves disturbeth him not."

—Aristotle

"The bad news is time flies. The good news is you're the pilot."
—Michael Althusier

Liz—the Pie Lady

Urban Edge Farm, Cranston, Rhode Island.

Sweet Potatoes.

Sungold tomatoes.

Green tomatoes for green tomato pie.

We met Liz at a hootenanny celebrating the fiftieth birthday of a mutual friend. (We realized we were dating ourselves when a friend asked us, "*What's a hootenanny?*") We started talking with Liz, and for some reason, our conversation turned to rocks, one of our favorite subjects. She said something that intrigued us, and we knew we would like to get to know her. "*Rocks*", she said, "*speak really slowly. Sometimes it takes a whole week for them just to say one word.*"

Although a marine biologist by training, Liz has spent much of her personal and professional life working on farms. "*It's always been about the earth,*" she told us. Liz has a large garden on a piece of land being farmed cooperatively and organically called the Urban Edge Farm, an offshoot of the Southside Community Land Trust in Providence, Rhode Island. So far, Liz has planted a few annual crops for her business. She makes a green tomato pie from an old antique Southern recipe she found. She makes a sun gold tomato pie, a squash pie, a pumpkin pie, and a ground cherry pie. It changes with the seasons. Liz sells her pies at a local farmer's market and by special order.

She loves hand tools, but,

> "*If it were up to me and time didn't matter I would take a broad fork and build one bed at a time until after ten years I would have the whole thing planted. That's where the rocks come in. They give me perspective. The permanency of them throughout the season has been a grounding influence. At first, they seemed like an obstacle and a hardship but then, as the season went by and I started to ask them what was the meaning of all this, I started to see it in a different way. They gave give me a sense of perspective. That I don't have to be instantaneously successful. I can work at it year by year. The granite gave me that.*"

Liz sells her pies at a local farmer's market in Providence, Rhode Island.

Thea —Hammer Fit, Dry Stack Stone Mason

Thea rocks! Lamoille County, Vermont.
Photo courtesy of Robyn Alvin

We discovered this amazing stonework on a lovely old farm in Vermont. We obviously had to meet the artist—here she is. Lamoille County, Vermont. *Photo courtesy of Robyn Alvin*

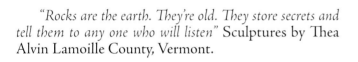

"Rocks are the earth. They're old. They store secrets and tell them to any one who will listen" Sculptures by Thea Alvin Lamoille County, Vermont.

How could we not want to hear the story of someone named Thea Sunshine by her Grateful Dead-following parents? We discovered her amazing stonework as we were moving part-time to Vermont and needed a washer/dryer at the only Sears located within miles of our new place. When we drove by her 60s-feeling farm and saw the stone piece in front of her house, we hit the brakes, turned around and just stood in front of her home. There was a key in the door with a note telling one of her friends to go in but we didn't feel this included us just yet. Later, we caught up with Thea and asked her about her obvious connection to stone. Here's what she said:

"Rocks are the earth. They're old. They store secrets and tell them to any one who will listen. Some of us can hear them when they speak. I'm one of those people. I gather stones together and assemble from what I see to be a natural chaos, a pattern, an order. Each rock has a flavor and an individual essence and gives it up to become part of a whole, more massive energy when assembled with others, having a new and exposed personality. When I work with rocks, I feel that I join my energy to theirs and hold the shape of all of them suspended in my head. There's a tremendous amount of emotion there buzzing around in my mind. And so, in a dance, the rocks and I sing and hum, conversing about who is next and which direction is best and which side is up. There are no wrong answers. When feeling your way along it feels right and so it is. I see the space that needs a rock on the wall or structure I'm working on. I examine its shape and turn to my pile of rocks. The only rock I see is the one that fits there in that space. The untouched piles of rocks become dull and seem far away. The stone that fits is singing to me, glowing. The rest wait their turn, patiently, as they always have.

It's a rare moment when I am calm and don't need the stones to settle my heart. The rocks are always there and they are always willing when I ask them to hold my pain. They cleanse my pain and make it beautiful. They keep my secrets.

I try not to fight them but sometimes the rocks don't want to go together. They refuse, I struggle, and the whole piece is reluctant and more likely to fail. I've learned to leave it, to turn and walk away. It's better to come another day when things are more settled.

So far, I've worked without mortar or pins, without manufactured means to keep the pieces and parts together. They are organic constructions and are meant to fall apart some time and go back to where they came from.

I rejoice that these stones and I can speak!"

Having a true presence where we find ourselves in each moment, whether in the garden or life in general, is a good and efficient way to get where we want to go. Our main objective in our own gardens was to create a garden that balanced and soothed our psyches. We believed that nature in general, and gardens in particular, are places where communication with our understanding of the Great Mystery is facilitated in unspoken ways. There is no need for language in the garden. The communication is intuitive and immediate. Because we wanted to experience "peace" on a daily basis we felt creating gardens where both we and the visitors to our nursery and gardens could come, walk around, sit, read a book, paint, talk to a friend, and experience "peace," without the burden of dogma, ideology, and anything else that separates human beings, was a good place to start. A good point of attraction for what we wanted to experience.

So, if we're living somewhere we'd rather not, if our garden is too big, too small, too close to the house, too far away, too shady, too sunny, we live in an apartment, etc., the first step toward moving forward is to assess where we are now, work with what we have and be grateful for whatever pleasure or joy comes with that moment. One positive experience draws another in what many call an attraction-based universe. And, our experience has been that life keeps getting better and better. As we think, so it is.

"The past is solid, the future is liquid."
— J.L. Aubert

Water

Betwys-y-Coed, Wales. *Photo courtesy of Alan & Elizabeth Taylor*

"As a lotus flower is born in water, grows in water and rises out of water to stand above it unsoiled, so I, born in the world, raised in the world having overcome the world, live unsoiled by the world." —Buddha Staffordshire, Derbyshire and Cheshire, England. *Photo courtesy of Alan & Elizabeth Taylor*

"We can hold back neither the coming of the flowers nor the downward rush of the stream; sooner or later, everything comes to its fruition." —Loy Ching-Yuen Bela krajina, Croatia. *Photo courtesy of Jonny Baker*

Water has been the central feature of gardens the world over for centuries, and responsible for the genesis of garden design. It is the following, simple question that has decided how gardens have taken their form since the beginning: How do we get the water to the plants? Followed by: How do we keep the water from running away? Or depending on your bioregion, how do we keep the water from flooding our garden?

Sacred springs, sacred rivers, sacred pools are at the heart of pilgrimages predating Christianity. Strattford, Ontario Canada. *Photo courtesy of Darlene Greydanus*

If you build a pond, they will come. Bristol County, Massachusetts.

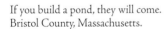

"In rivers, the water that you touch is the last of what has passed and the first of that which comes; so with present time." —Leonardo da Vinci. *Photo courtesy of Sandra Serretti*

One of the earliest water features built at Seven Arrows Farm. Children are drawn to it like a bowl of candy. Bristol County, Massachusetts.

We keep building ponds; one year a wood duck took up residence in this one for a week in the fall. Another spring we found a dozen wood duck chicks toodling around without a mom. When she didn't show by dark, we sent them to a waterfowl rehabilitator. They were on their way flying north a few weeks after being rehabilitated. Bristol County, Massachusetts.

Cornwall, England. *Photo courtesy of Carolyn Heathcote*

But before this, water was at the heart of the creation stories of the world's major religions. The book of Genesis in the Judeo-Christian story speaks of water as a primordial element (Genesis 1:1-6). The Koran also speaks of this. *We have created every living thing from water.* (Koran 21:30.) A Blackfoot Indian creation story speaks of the time when a "great womb" with all the animals within it, burst and everything was under water.

*"I am not quite sure whether I am dreaming or remembering, whether I have lived my life or dreamed it. Just as dreams do, memory makes me profoundly aware of the unreality, the evanescence of the world, a fleeting image in the moving water." —*Eugene Ionesco. *Photo courtesy of Florence Blanchetierre*

"Water sustains all."
—Thales of Miletus. 600 BC

Water has been considered "sacred" from ancient history right on through to modern times. Sacred springs, sacred rivers, sacred pools are at the heart of pilgrimages predating Christianity. Ancient Babylonians, Greeks, Romans, and Celts all assigned gods and goddesses to sacred springs, rivers, pools, and wells, attributing healing powers both to the deity and the water.

When humans lived in huts enclosed by a brush fence for protection, the water source would often be found inside the enclosure. Either ditches for irrigation or paths to and from the water source served as the initial force and structure defining and dividing the space inside the enclosure. In places that were flat and open, canals and ditches took on a straight-line approach. These evolved into the straight runnels of the classic Persian garden, and the canals of Holland. In areas that were mountainous, rocky, or otherwise rugged terrain, the ditches and canals would be accompanied by terracing with both canal and terrace conforming to the existing landscape, following the contours of the mountainside for instance. In either instance, form followed function, and the layout of the farm and garden was dictated by the ease of accessing and controlling the crucial element necessary for successful plant growth, and indeed human survival—water.

"What makes a river so restful to people is that it doesn't have any doubt—it is sure to get where it is going, and it doesn't want to go anywhere else."
—Hal Boyle

These clients asked for a special rock to be placed out into the pond so they could sit on it for meditation. Bristol County, Massachusetts.

Is it any wonder that water obviously plays a central role in our gardens of today? We pay more for property with a view of any body of water. Riverview, lake view, water view are all magical words to a real estate agent. So why do we value properties that have a view of the water more than other properties? Who knows?

Whatever mysterious power water has, there's no question that it's inclusion in a garden can enhance the experience of a gardener seeking peace.

"If there is magic on the planet, it is contained in the water."
—Loren Eisley

Aroma

Aromatherapists are familiar with the connection between the limbic system of the brain and aroma. Judy counts herself as one of them having taken various aromatherapy certification courses over the years. She has been a "lurker" on many internet chat lists involving both psychotherapeutic and medicinal uses of essential oils. Her collection of oils number in the hundreds. She and her friends spend many Sunday afternoons in the winter passing around their newest finds for the joy of smelling them!

Before that, however, we were gardeners and, like many gardeners, Judy considered her favorite plants those that smelled good. Gardeners in India choose their plants for fragrance as much as anything else. Not so much here in the U. S. We seem to be attracted more to color and texture. The connection between sweet smells and the divine predates the Bible. The scent of flowers often announced the presence of Indian sages and masters. Even today, some of our Hindu friends have spoken to us of this first-hand experience.

Aroma is known to both calm and uplift at the same time. Incense has been used for these purposes and to increase awareness of the divine since the time of the early Christian churches. Somewhere along the line, "evil" took on its own smell as well. Some historical references speak of sulphur as the smell of the devil.

It is an accepted medical fact that the limbic system of the brain controls emotions, memory, and metabolism to a certain degree. So clearly, what you smell can influence how you feel. Smell something pleasant and you feel good. Smell something bad and your mood declines. While certain aromas are given credit for influencing certain emotions or helping to create certain emotional experiences (calm, lift anger, soothe irritability, smooth emotional highs and lows, for example), newer research seems to indicate this can be a personal thing as well. Your sense of smell is unique to yourself, as unique as your fingerprint it is said. A study conducted with 2000 participants at Hamamatsu University in Japan concluded that diastolic blood pressure decreased twenty-four percent during exercise when participants inhaled an aroma of their choice (rose, sweet orange, lemon, peppermint, jasmine, or lavender). One obviously wants to plant material whose aromas uplift, not offend. Most gardeners, we think, habitually and instinctually rub the leaves or flowers of plants as they walk by. Is it scented, we wonder? We asked some of our friends what their favorite scented plants were and here's a partial list of what they liked.

Angel's Trumpets (Brumansias, Daturas), Bee Balms (Monarda didyma), Heliotropes (Heliotropium aborescens), Hostas (mostly the fragrant white flowering varieties), Lavenders (all of them!), Lilies (Lilium, especially some of the hybrid trumpet and oriental lilies), Lily-of-the Valley (Convarallia majalis), Peonies (Paeonia spp), Clove Pinks (Dianthus caryophyllus,D. gratianopolitanus) Flowering Tobacco (Nicotiana alata, sylvestris, suaveolens.), Scented Geraniums (Pelargonium) Stocks (Matthiola longipetala, incana), Sweet Peas (Lathyrus odoratus), Sweet Williams (Dianthus barbatus), Sweet Violet (Viola odorata), Herbs (practically all of them).

Practically everybody liked some of the fragrant Honeysuckles (Lonicera periclymenulsm, x. heckrottii, Jasmines (J. sambac and J. officinale), Moonflower (Ipomoea alba) Heirloom and old-fashioned Roses like R. sombreuil, Mme. Alfred Carriere, Zephirine Drouhin, fragrant Viburnums V.carlesii, Daphnes like (Daphne x. burkwoodii 'Carol Mackie' and 'Somerset'), Lilacs (Syringa) hundreds of them, and Sweet Pepperbush (Clethra alnifolia). These are some of the fragrant plants we can get away with here in New England. There are lots of others, of course.

A greenhouse plant we grow for interest sake, Amorphophallus konjac, is said to give off an aroma similar to rotting flesh; we call it "Stinky" and put up pictures of its unique flower on our web site when it blooms. "Stinky" is proud of its flowers and appreciates visits from the adoring public. One actually wintered over here outside in Zone 6 quite nicely to attract flies which are the sole pollinators of this plant.

Spearmint (Mentha spicata). *Photo courtesy of John Mewitt*

Lemon Balm (Melissa officinalis) and Lavender (Lavendula angustifolia). *Photo courtesy of Nicole Simoes*

Bee Balm (Monarda didyma). *"I took this photo on a warm June day meandering about the Arboretum where I frequently go to take photos. While it's not my garden, I do feel peaceful when I am there. I am a gardener too and find that gardening is very therapeutic in so many ways. I was diagnosed with fibromyalgia back in 2001, and was out of work for a year. The only thing that got me out of bed or off the sofa was my container garden I had on the second story porch of where I lived at the time. I would lose myself in what I was do-ing. I forgot about my pain for a little while. I know that nurturing those plants is what got me through that time and continued to help me regain my strength and health—mind, body, and spirit. As time went on, I moved from the container garden to a proper garden where I had to do more physical work to amend the soil and plant on a bigger scale. The larger and more beautiful my garden grew, the stronger and healthier I felt. Since then I have felt a deeper connection to nature and a sense of gratitude for how it helped me heal."* Greensboro, North Carolina. *Photo courtesy of Heidi Noëlle Schachtschneider*

"Yet, O thou beautiful rose! Queen rose so fair and sweet. What were lover or crown to thee, without the clay at thy feet?" Julia C R Dorr. Rosa "Sombreuil." Providence County, Rhode Island. *Photo courtesy of Hanaan Rosenthal*

"And I will make thee beds of roses And a thousand fragrant posies." —Christopher Marlow. Rosa "Flowergirl." Providence County, Rhode Island. *Photo courtesy of Hanaan Rosenthal*

"If the rose puzzled its mind over the question how it grew, it would not have been the miracle that it is." —J B Yeats, 1871-1957. Warwickshire, England. *Photo courtesy of Alan & Elizabeth Taylor*

Plants and People Connection

Do plants connect with people? Many people think they do. We spent a delightful afternoon one winter's Sunday listening to the story of two lovely Britons of Indian origin, a brother and sister, clearly connected to one another, although separated by the Atlantic Ocean. Finishing each other's sentences in flawless segue, they talked about their father's magical relationship to his plants.

"When he goes out to his gardens, he's often cross and grumpy. But when he returns he's full of joy. He often talks to the roses, especially the ones that are performing poorly. After conversing with them, he will move them to a new spot where inevitably they will thrive. I asked him what he was doing once and he said, 'Plants need to see their owner, feel that someone cares for them, listens to them. So I listen and they tell me what they need. Then I help them.' When he goes back to India, his plants start to waste away. It's as if they're pining away for him. As soon as he returns, within twenty-four hours, they're back, as vibrant as ever."

"When love first came to Earth, the Spring spread rose-beds to receive him." Thomas Campbell. Rosa "Ballerina." Providence County, Rhode Island. *Photo courtesy of Hanaan Rosenthal*

Photo courtesy of Hanaan Rosenthal

"*You are responsible, forever, for what you have tamed. You are responsible for your rose.*" Antoine de Saint-Expery. Providence County, Rhode Island.

"*The splendor of the rose and the whiteness of the lily do not rob the little violet of its scent nor the daisy of its simple charm. If every tiny flower wanted to be a rose, spring would lose its loveliness.*" Therese de Lisieux. Providence County, Rhode Island.

Rick's story

Judy's dad, Rick, who died in the spring of 2005, was an avid gardener for as long as she can remember. She remembers him spending most of each Saturday and Sunday during the growing season planting, transplanting, weeding, watering, heading out to the nursery in the next town and repeating the whole ritual. Their small property was dominated by a 1950s-style ranch house, requisite lawn and Rick's landscape. Lots of green, not too much color. Later, he and Judy's mom moved to Judy's grandparents' house, a block away from the Long Island Sound in the small Connecticut town where the whole family grew up. More space, a larger palette to work with, but Rick never did anything terrifically creative with the expanded area—just the same planting, a few things here, a few things there and the like. Planting, weeding, watering, transplanting. The property was dominated by beech trees, one huge beech in particular. When the beech finally came down after several years of losing bits and pieces of itself in winds and storms, Judy's mom said she didn't care about the house where she was born any more. She was ready to move, and off they went to an assisted living community in Florida.

Charley? Ontario, Canada. *Photo courtesy of Mary A. Smith*

If Rick had been born in the forties or fifties, instead of 1915, and returned from the Vietnam Era War, instead of World War II, he probably would have been diagnosed with Post Traumatic Stress Disorder. A handsome war hero he lived his peak life experience driving tanks through Europe. War causes ordinary men to do extraordinary things, and after it some men thrive, some men fail to thrive, and some lead ordinary lives of quiet acceptance. Rick never really got it together to repeat that peak experience in civilian life. He was probably somewhere between "failure to thrive" and "quiet acceptance." He spent his life working a series of jobs that never excited him and retired early after being laid-off from the last in the series. He spent the rest of his life gardening or doing crossword puzzles. Overall, he was still a good dad, although impossible to know in any meaningful way.

He did one thing that was impressive, however. He would walk out to the deck of his house in Connecticut, call "Charley" and soon a squirrel would come down out of the trees and sit on his shoulder. The two of them would sit quietly together while Rick worked on his crossword puzzle, passing Charley a peanut occasionally. One "Charley" would be followed by another and then another over the years. Several years ago, a sparrow came down and sat on Judy's shoulder at an outdoor café. It hopped back and forth from her finger to her shoulder for about an hour. She said, "*This must be what I got from Dad.*"

For the most part, Rick didn't communicate with Judy. But he didn't communicate with anyone, so she didn't take it personally. At one point, she sent him a questionnaire where he could check responses to questions about his life, feelings, etc. Judy hoped it would elicit a response, which could serve as a starting point for a closer relationship, but he never returned or mentioned it. Neither did she. Later, when we started the nursery, Rick would drive the two hours from Connecticut to our home in Massachusetts, work all day in our infant business, planting, weeding, and laying bricks, all the while wheezing and coughing from his emphysema brought on by his pack-a-day Camel's habit. We would have lunch, work some more, and then he would drive home. Not much chatting. *"What's blooming down at your place, Dad?" "Not too much. The same things you've got here."* The most intimate conversation Judy ever had with him was when she asked him why he spent so much time gardening. *"It's a quiet place,"* he said, *"where my mind's my own, where I can rest."* Then she asked, *"Dad, have you ever seen what some folks call "nature spirits, you know, little elves or fairies?" "Yes,"* he said, *"out of the corner of my eye, darting around."*

Before he moved to Florida, Rick gave Judy a silver heart necklace. On the first anniversary of his death, she found a nearly identical silver heart on the patio he built for us.

> *"O Lord, grant that in some way it may rain every day, say from about midnight until three o'clock in the morning, but, you see, it must be gentle and warm so that it can soak in; grant that at the same time it would not rain on campion, alyssum, helianthemum, lavender, and the others which you in your infinite wisdom know are drought loving plants—I will write their names on a paper if you like—and grant that the sun may shine the whole day long, but not everywhere (not for instance, on spiraea, or on gentian, plantain lily and the rhododendron), and not too much; that there may be plenty of dew and little wind, enough worms, no plant lice and snails, no mildew, and that once a week thin liquid manure and guano may fall from heaven. Amen."*
> —Karel Capek

Margaret's Memorial Garden

When we asked Margaret how she wanted us to describe her, she asked her friends to help. They called her "a woman fulfilled through gardening", "a strong woman", "the glue that holds her family together" among other things. She is also the owner of a small business.

"We never used the backyard much but for years, I would say to Jacinto, 'I want a garden.' 'We'll start it next year, I promise,' he would say. When he got so sick I said, 'I guess I'm never going to get my garden.' As sick as he was he would tell me, 'Next year, Margarita. We'll start it next year.' Before Jacinto died, he told me he would try to come back to let me know he was in heaven with Jesus. The night he died, a white moth got into our house. It stayed in the house with us until the day we buried him. Five days the moth was in my kitchen on the screen door. It could have left many times. The door was opened and closed a lot during that five-day period. The day we buried Jacinto, the moth was very weak. I cried because I knew the moth would be dead when I got back to the house. I really believe this moth was Jacinto's spirit telling us he was okay and in heaven. I saved the moth and have it in a garden terrarium with some trees.

"About a year after Jacinto died, I got some income tax money back. It was the first time ever. The kids wanted me to spend it on a vacation. 'Where am I going to go that I'll enjoy?' I asked them. 'My Jacinto isn't here.' So I went to a garden center and they recommended two women to help. It's a small yard but I had a vision for it— flowers, all over. I wanted it in memory of my Jacinto. They researched Biblical plants. We planted bleeding hearts and I have a Blessed Virgin Mary statue, a gift from Mercedes, Jacinto's sister-in-law. Every day I'm out in that garden. I'm really at peace there. 'So Jacinto', I said, 'I finally got my garden.' Sometimes when the plants move in the breeze I think, maybe that's Jacinto blowing by. He was a wonderful man, my soul mate. We were married twenty-seven years.

"Jacinto did manage to come to me in his own time and way. I find that when I am at my worst he comes to me in some way. I miss him so much every day, some more than others. I wish my garden was still in bloom in the fall and winter. I could always take a walk out back and find him along the way somewhere."

Providence County, Rhode Island. *Photo courtesy of Stewart Martin*

108

Providence County, Rhode Island. *Photo courtesy of Stewart Martin*

Providence County, Rhode Island. *Photo courtesy of Stewart Martin*

Providence County, Rhode Island. *Photo courtesy of Stewart Martin*

Providence County, Rhode Island.

When it became clear Jacinto was going to die, he and Margaret went to a sculptor and had mold made of their hands clasped together. Providence County, Rhode Island.

John—Artist

We've known John forever, and he very graciously displays some of his work in our gardens. We asked John to describe his garden for us.

"As a ceramic artist, as well as a gardener, I find myself doubly involved in acts of the sacred. For me, the most exciting part of the garden is when I get to have my hands in the earth. In addition, this explains my passion with clay in the studio. The coolness of the earth, the countless organisms swarming before me heighten my attention as I carefully move the earth in order to place a new plant into its perfect spot. My fingers become like roots in the earth as they slowly move in to make way for a new addition. One of my favorite spots is actually outside the garden. It is my second story window. Looking down at the garden from above is very advantageous, as it offers me an overall vista of the space. I get to watch the garden taking shape over the course of the season, filling in, colors blending, fading, textures merging, in a cacophony of symphonic orchestration that I have so little to do with. I planted a Paul's Himalayan climbing rose near the shed and it is now crawling all over the roof. This second story view is perfect for watching the unfolding of the tiny pink roses slowly spreading out, turning the inanimate into the animate. Walking downstairs and going out into the garden I walk onto the weathered, circular brick patio with its semi circular stuccoed and hand-tiled retaining wall and seat with ceramic tiled cover. I am now two feet below the garden looking up. A wall of ornamental grasses interspersed with Hollywood Junipers and Holly, Russian Giant Cannas and mammoth Caster bean plants spotted with Verbena Buonariensis, Perilla, Hollyhock, Rudbeckia and Coreopsis, stands in front of me. You can feel and hear the rustling of the grasses as the afternoon winds come in off the bay and move through the tall Oak and then the garden. Sometimes I lie in a hammock on the patio, closing my eyes to allow all of the other senses to take over. Gardening for me is an act of God.

"My work with clay/ceramics comes right out of the garden. During graduate school, I decided to unify my passions in the garden with those of clay. My ceramic work would be for and about the garden. Functional sculpture is what I call it. I took the inspirations I found from gardening and transferred them into my work with clay. Using natural as well as man-made scenes of gardens I shaped my work into an organic commentary, which allows the work to rest into a garden space.

"I hold a piece of clay in my hand, gently squeezing, rolling and stretching it into a long coil. I press its soft, pliable form that easily responds to my touch. I add this coil to another and watch as hunk becomes form, as smooth becomes texture. The movement of my hands, my eyes, and my body is a reaction of the movement in my mind. The work is growing before me, and I feel a thrill as each new stage arrives. I adjust, correct, and prod the piece toward that which I hold in my imagination. The vision and the work unfold before me, as they become one. This process, of head to hand, is for me the breath of life. It's exciting to feel an idea forming and then to realize that idea as an object. To watch a piece taking shape, while my whole being is engaged in the act of creation, is reward enough for me.

"I have chosen the garden as my canvas on which I continually paint my ideas. I make garden objects that help enliven the space, creating dynamic interactions or quiet moments. I want to give the viewer a time to pause, reflect, think, and make them smile."

"So if you'll permit, a little advice from two who have felt passion's sting: if you invite art into the garden, be prepared for a lesson on love. It seems only right that we learn love's lessons here; relationship is so evident in a garden. Above the hum of ecosystems, life webs, and companion plantings, the gods whisper. True love, whether romantic or platonic, brotherly, sisterly, for friend or humanity, transcends the physical. It seeks a higher image of the human being. It is not a feeling. It is an infinite force that speaks of the unity of life and the interconnectedness of all things. So go ahead, invite art into the garden, but go thoughtfully, prayerfully even, and stay firmly rooted in the divine, for you are treading on passionate ground."

—Spring Gillard

"As a ceramic artist, as well as a gardener, I find myself doubly involved in acts of the sacred. My work with clay/ceramics comes right out of the garden." Providence County, Rhode Island.

Providence County, Rhode Island.

Providence County, Rhode Island.

Providence County, Rhode Island.

Providence County, Rhode Island.

"I planted a Paul's Himalayan climbing rose near the shed and it is now crawling all over the roof. This second story view is perfect for watching the unfolding of the tiny pink roses slowly spreading out, turning the inanimate into the animate." Providence County, Rhode Island.

Providence County, Rhode Island.

Johanne—Gardener

We asked Johanne how she wanted to be described and she said "gardener." We know her to be a beautiful, fascinating, multilingual, home-schooling mom, whose very avant-garde parents took her all over the world as a child, providing her with some great fodder for stories to be told as an adult!

"Each year we get anxious when we see the mama raccoon walking across the yard and climbing the large maple in our yard. March. April. May. Where is her new litter? Did something happen to her? Is she through having litters? Each Spring I pull out my old garden journals and read off the dates of past "first-sightings" of our raccoon-lets. Soothed by the disparate dates in my journal we settle into spring and wait for first sightings. In mid-summer, we write down the first time she teaches them to forage in the garden. For some reason she is partial to using ferns in this foraging class. She wraps her dainty paws around a fern and tugs. She peers into the hole and then returns the fern, more or less, to its spot. Each of her babies then tries in turn. When the lesson is over, I replant whatever she has uprooted in her lessons. Sometimes they practice for a whole week. A whole week of being honored by this diligent mother and her terribly charming babies.

We asked Johanne how she wanted to be described and she said "gardener." *Photo courtesy of Hanaan Rosenthal*

"When we first brought the kids to our new property, they were downcast when they saw just how dreary these two half-abandoned buildings looked. The two ramshackle buildings were peeling and covered in thick vines of poison ivy. I took the kids into the back yard, which is large for a city garden. The whole back yard was covered with a thick layer of red, gold, brown, and orange leaves. They asked for rakes. We spent an hour grimly raking leaves from around all seven cars that were parked in the yard including a rusting tractor. They were quiet and I felt that this move was going to be an unfair burden on them. Once we had finished, the kids threw down their rakes and leapt into the pile. They grabbed armfuls of golden leaves, threw them into the air screaming, "we're rich!" Armful after armful of autumn leaves. They were filled with joy. The falling-apart houses no longer mattered, moving from our beloved house, leaving our old neighborhood. All was softened. Three maple trees. Suddenly we were rich.

Providence County,
Rhode Island.

Providence County,
Rhode Island.

118

Providence County, Rhode Island. *Photo courtesy of Johanne Rosenthal*

Providence County, Rhode Island. *Photo courtesy of Johanne Rosenthal*

Providence County, Rhode Island. *Photo courtesy of Johanne Rosenthal*

Providence County, Rhode Island. *Photo courtesy of Johanne Rosenthal*

Providence County, Rhode Island. *Photo courtesy of Johanne Rosenthal*

"We have had a first-day-of-spring ritual with three of the kids' friends since they were all tiny. Nathan, Devon, and Rose come over the night before spring. That night they go to sleep knowing that in the morning they will wake up together at sunrise in Springtime. We breakfast, dye Easter eggs with onionskins and turmeric, tea, and red cabbage. We plant seeds and I read them stories about old spring rituals. The first year in our new house my then-four-year-old son ran out into the yard at daybreak, made a lap around the yard and returned to me crest fallen. 'Where are all the crocuses?' he asked. He had been sure the yard would be carpeted in flowers. I ran out to the supermarket and bought all the daffodils and pansies I could afford, which were not many. When I told the man at the florist counter why I was buying them, he sent me home with flats of free spring flowers. We spent that morning planting in the cold wakening earth.

"A couple of months before we moved I had an accident that changed my vision permanently and added the risk of complications later. Everything had changed for me. The world I saw now was muddied. I was torn apart on a deep level. I wanted to curl up and be left alone. That wasn't an option. We were moving, selling our home, renovating our new house, and I was home schooling the kids. We moved in February. Spring began in April. That summer I threw any extra time I had into the yard, a large rectangle of gravel that had been used for parking for forty years. I would go out after dinner and rake gravel in the dark. I was fighting for any shred of peace or distraction. I wanted a garden of blues, pinks, apricots and silvers, softness and laciness, gentle winds, and white flowers that would glow in the dark. I wanted no flower that screamed, 'Look at me!' I wanted shade and sunlight, boulders that would warm and comfort anyone who sat with them, paths that were too narrow, too twisty, where you had to take the time to avoid flowers spilling over the paths. Roses on bowers and columbines nodding, and hidden statues that rewarded you if you took the time to peak under the gooseberry bushes. I searched for harmony in the garden and that summer as I shuffled to the eye doctor with each new emergency, I returned home to the garden that only I could see.

"My least favorite/favorite spot in the yard is a huge deep hole that Olivia, Aylam, and their friends have dug these past four years. They dig in all seasons. They dig and they talk. This hole has grown as large as the kids themselves have. They sit and excavate and discuss everything. They untie their worries and leave them in the hole. They wear themselves out in the hole. This hole is large and ugly and I have planted a semicircle flowerbed on one side to camouflage it. But there is no hiding a four-foot crater in a city garden. They've used clay from the hole to make bowls. They've crushed rocks to magical rock dust. They've roasted marshmallows in fires over the hole. They've fought and made up in that hole. When all games are spent and boredom overwhelms, someone will say, 'Let's go dig.' And away they go. One day I'll plant a tree in the hole or fill it in. Or maybe I'll keep it and dig when my heart is all tied up.

"The most amazing single moment for me was when I heard my apple tree gasp. I had been gone for a month and a wild rose and grape vine (both being opportunists) had taken advantage and engulfed a small apple tree. I took the better part of a morning untwining them and setting them back on the fence. The moment I removed the last heavy curtain of vine, the apple tree shuddered and took a deep breath. The kind that a newborn makes on his first try."

"They sit and excavate and discuss everything. They untie their worries and leave them in the hole. One day I'll plant a tree in the hole or fill it in. Or maybe I'll keep it and dig when my heart is all tied up." Providence County, Rhode Island. *Photo courtesy of Hanaan Rosenthal*

Aquilegia "Nora Barlow." Providence County, Rhode Island. *Photo courtesy of Hanaan Rosenthal*

Providence County, Rhode Island.
Photo courtesy of Hanaan Rosenthal

Centauria Montana. Providence County, Rhode Island.
Photo courtesy of Hanaan Rosenthal

Hydrangea "Nikko Blue." Providence County, Rhode
Island. *Photo courtesy of Hanaan Rosenthal*

Providence County, Rhode Island.
Photo courtesy of Hanaan Rosenthal

Providence County, Rhode Island.
Photo courtesy of Hanaan Rosenthal

Providence County, Rhode Island.
Photo courtesy of Hanaan Rosenthal

Providence County, Rhode Island.
Photo courtesy of Hanaan Rosenthal

Providence County, Rhode Island. *Photo courtesy of Hanaan Rosenthal*

Providence County, Rhode Island.
Photo courtesy of Hanaan Rosenthal

Providence County, Rhode Island.
Photo courtesy of Hanaan Rosenthal

Providence County, Rhode Island. *Photo courtesy of Hanaan Rosenthal*

Providence County, Rhode Island.
Photo courtesy of Hanaan Rosenthal

Nancy - Telecommunication Manager

"I always had some type of houseplants, but nothing overwhelming. When I first moved to Yonkers and lived with my mother, I had a small garden in the yard. Not a lot, just something to mess around with. In 1997, I bought the condominium unit next door and I started container gardening. Not the amount I have now. I had maybe twenty-five pots or so. Each year I'd add a little more. In 2002, when a relationship ended, I went wild. Gardening became my therapy. Coming home from work, I'd go out into my yard and putter 'round for hours. Each year after that I'd add more pots, more plants.

"I love going out and just sitting in my garden. I look around and spot something that needs deadheading or a trim. I pop out of my seat, tend to it, and look around for something else that needs attention. Each year I try something new—vines, pumpkins, grasses. One year a friend who was moving to California brought me over twenty more plants— as if I didn't have enough! I had done a lot of planning on how I was going to arrange things.

"I draw a plan each year. I try to create paths, as if I had acreage, rather than four hundred square feet.

"On weekends or days off, I like sitting at my table with my morning paper, breakfast, and a mug of coffee. That's the best time. It's quiet. The only sound is the birds. I am on a busy street and once the traffic starts flowing, it can get noisy—especially when a bus or fire truck passes. My other favorite spot is on the bench in the back. During the afternoon in the summer, it is too hot to sit there. But as the sun goes down, or in the morning, it's a wonderful spot to sit and enjoy my garden.

"It takes me about an hour to water everything. I find that to be a great way to unwind when I come home from work. I love how all the bees and wasps land to drink the water on the wet leaves. I was upset this year when a visitor (I don't know if it was a raccoon or opossum) ate all my peppers and most of my tomatoes. I love wildlife, but I was really looking forward to those peppers!

"I love my yard. I sometimes wish I had places to plant in the ground. But, all in all, I am happy on my little piece of the planet."

Yonkers, New York. *Photo courtesy of Nancy Foote*   Yonkers, New York. *Photo courtesy of Nancy Foote*

Yonkers, New York. *Photo courtesy of Nancy Foote*

Yonkers, New York. *Photo courtesy of Nancy Foote*

Nancy took one photo a week all season. We took about every other one for this layout. Yonkers, New York. *Photos courtesy of Nancy Foote*

"An addiction to gardening is not all bad when you consider all the other choices in life."

—Cora Lea Bell

Barbara—Garden Writer

Newport County, Rhode Island. *Photo courtesy of Danya Martin*

"When I look out of the window at my 'landscape', I see a sorry sight—a garden in a state of perpetual neglect. I spend so much time writing about gardening and what gardeners should be doing that I don't have time to be doing any of it in my own garden. My garden both glowers at me as I pass by and then looks pathetic—like a puppy dog when you're not paying attention! I have a very visceral relationship with my garden. Contrary to the idyllic picture of gardening as a calming pursuit, mine is like a volatile marriage. Sometimes I love my garden and sometimes I don't! Sometimes I put lots of love and attention into it and sometimes not. And it shows! I can pray in my garden and I can vent in my garden.

"My garden is a very personal reflection of me—for good or ill. One walk around my garden would reveal a whole host of aspects of my personality some of which I should probably keep hidden but it's out there for all to see—if you can read it.

"I do particularly love the shade bed. The one garden probably gets the least attention but doesn't mind. It continues to look tranquil in the dappled shade. I like foliage almost better than I like blossoms. Such subtle variety of color and texture, sort of understated elegance and not so showy."

Bristol County, Massachusetts.

Kalmia latifolia "Raspberry Glow." Hosta "Piglit." Bristol County, Massachusetts.

Phil - Musician, Peace Activist, and "Bodhisattva" to Some

    Phil writes a lot of music. He is, or has been, a member of practically every Celtic or wild folk band in Providence, Rhode Island. He has also been gardening at the Southside Community Land Trust for over thirteen years. He often writes music to remind people and himself to *"notice the beauty in our lives when we look at the sky, a tree, a flower, a person. To really look and enjoy them."* One of the groups he plays with released a CD entitled, *To the Dance Floor.* If you brought a gnome (it didn't have to be a living one) to the CD release party at a local coffee house, you got in free.

Phil—Bodhisattva. *Photo courtesy of Lucas Folia Photography*

*Courtesy of
Sheila Bocchine*

Photo courtesy of Lucas Foglia Photography

"*Years ago, I was living in Omaha when our neighborhood was transformed by a community garden. The garden was started on a vacant lot as an antidote to the despair we were feeling in the wake of five murders in one month. Gardeners know the powerful medicine gardens can be. Within six months, our neighborhood changed. We'd met each other, most for the first time. We made new friends and saw the real immediate effects of our shared labor, and we felt safer for it, deeply so.*" Katherine Brown, Director, Southside Community Land Trust.

Photo courtesy of Lucas Foglia Photography

Photo courtesy of Lucas Foglia Photography

Photo courtesy of Lucas Foglia Photography

Photo courtesy of Lucas Foglia Photography

Photo courtesy of Lucas Foglia Photography

Photo courtesy of Lucas Foglia Photography

Sheila's Story—Sister, Presentation Order

We met Sheila years ago when she spent sabbatical time at a monastery near us in Massachusetts. During breaks in her program, she would come and spend hours reading, writing and chatting with us in our tearoom. We became great friends and have stayed in touch over the years. She lives in the Blue Mountains west of Sydney. As well as being Social Justice Coordinator for her Congregation, Presentation Sisters Wagga, her passion is "The Universe Story" and the journey this has taken her on, especially in her own spirituality.

In addition to her garden, Sheila's passion is 'The Universe Story' and the journey this has taken her on, especially in her own spirituality. Wagga, Australia. *Photo courtesy of Sheila Quonoey*

"I live in the Blue Mountains of Australia. Tall gum trees, with thick trunks and branches that bend in the wind, surround my home. I feel protected by these tall 'guards.' I've created a Peace Garden in memory of a friend who died. It has pebbles, stepping stones, ferns, water bowls and a lantern. There's a birdbath, and posters of Green Tara and Aboriginal legends. Through my back doors, I look onto a courtyard where I have planted mostly Australian trees that are native to the area. They attract birds and butterflies. My plan was to create a space of stillness and peace. A Tibetan Buddha sits near a birdbath. A statue of Quan Yin rests on the large rocks and speaks of mercy and compassion. Four women of various stances stand on a flat rock of sandstone. These women are named "Vigiling Women," and represent a place of groundedness, and focus for me. There's a worm farm and beautiful lavenders, hibiscus, roses, and camellias."

"My plan was to create a space of stillness and peace." Wagga, Australia. *Photo courtesy of Sheila Quonoey*

Wagga, Australia. *Photo courtesy of Sheila Quonoey*

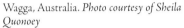

Wagga, Australia. *Photo courtesy of Sheila Quonoey*

Wagga, Australia. *Photo courtesy of Sheila Quonoey*

"When I first arrived in Wagga, I had a special 'friend' who lived just behind my fence. It was a She Oak or Casuarina, which is native to Australia. She hung over my fence and we became good friends. Sadly, she became diseased and was chopped down. I wrote a poem about her."

Wagga, Australia. *Photo courtesy of Sheila Quonoey*

She Oak

She stands
Just behind my fence.
Would I, could I
Stand in her world.

Knowing, feeling
What it was like
Hanging all day,
All night
Letting go
Just hanging.

Welcoming the wind
As she plays with
Her strands
Weaving in and out
The branches:
Kicking, tossing, dancing
Like a well-trained gymnast.
Overhearing conversation
Of a family of doves
Who gather each morning,
Enjoying the colour of the
Parrots: the chatter of the
Yellow-crested cockatoos
And the singing of Magpie
And Kookaburra.

Feeling life surge through
Her veins.
As the rain washes her needles
Soaks into the soil
Where eager roots
Drink and she is refreshed.

As she shakes and rids herself
Of old twigs and leaves
She laughs to herself
Knowing Sheila
Will once more fetch the
Broom and gather together
Her droppings.
It is a relationship
Which slowly grows.

Resistance is Futile

Somewhere back in the early nineties, the thirty-five acres of woods, meadows, and wetlands behind our property, which had been described to us as "undevelopable" when we bought the property in the seventies, suddenly became developable, or at least potentially so. The family who owned the property decided they would begin the process of pursuing the re-zoning of the land to accommodate what seemed to us a great number of homes pushed tight up against each other and up against us.

This possibility consumed us, particularly Judy. She would have nightmare after nightmare involving the developer and our loss of the quiet beauty of the land surrounding us and its wildlife residents we had grown accustomed to. Judy would cry and eventually stopped walking on the property altogether. The potential loss of such beauty and the displacement of deer, fox, coyotes, and the other residents was too much for her. It became her greatest fear and source of anxiety. When the developer began the legal processes needed to complete his plans, we found ourselves pushing against this with all our might. For ten years we pushed. All this pushing and resisting kept it front and center in our consciousness. We were exhausted. Eventually, something changed within the local city governance and the developers were given permission to proceed.

The development of the property was very hard for us to see and hear. But we no longer had an adversary. In fact, they were very respectful to us, accommodating when they could be and, in general, being what we would have to call "good winners." We approached them about letting us plant a border of fast growing evergreens along the property lines, more suitable than the normal landscape material they were used to using on their jobs. We received a substantial check for the plants even before we needed to pay our supplier. And, (and this is a big "and") they agreed to give seventeen of the original acres to be preserved as a nature trail.

When we look back on all those events, we realize we were always a little discomforted by our actions. Yes, we believed our "cause" was the higher one, one of greater good for many reasons. Doesn't one usually believe their cause is the nobler? And they believed that they should be able to do what they wanted with their property. Can't fault them for that! If we won, it clearly meant them losing, a scenario that did not match our philosophy that everyone needed to win. Looking back, it is obvious to us now that we did not trust that all things would work out for the best. Yet, that is clearly, what happened. This was a hard lesson in letting go and trusting in the true benevolence of the Universe.

Resistance is futile.

True Things About Creating a Sanctuary Garden

- Your garden reflects back to you your own energy. You are where you are. This is neither good nor bad. It simply is.
- If you don't like what you see, look around for something you do like. Imitate it if you like. There's probably not too much that hasn't been done somewhere before, so don't think you have to re-invent any wheels. Let other people's gardens or wild places serve as muses if you like. You'll put your own spin on it just because you are a unique human being.
- As you grow and change, so will your garden.
- You will never get it done. It (you) will want to add things, move things around a bit, and remove things. That's good. You're not dead yet!
- Remember you are not the only inhabitants of your space. The rocks, trees, flowers, insects, and microorganisms all have life and are conduits of pure, positive energy. They are never out of sync with their true natures. The earth really is in good hands.
- Go with the flow. If it's right, it's easy. It's simple. It's peaceful.
- It is all about you.
- Say "thank you" a lot.
- Life is meant to be fun. If it's not fun, don't do it.
- There are no rules.

Returning to the Garden of Eden.
Perhaps the story of humankind's expulsion from the Garden of Eden (Paradise) after the feminine, feeling side of creation (Eve) is tempted by knowledge and thought (Snake and the Apple), represents nothing more than humankind's disconnect with Pure, Positive Energy, God, by replacing feeling with thought. How do we get back? Connect with positive feelings. Connect with joy, easy as that. That is our theory, at least.

Dayenu

"The colors of the rainbow so pretty in the sky Are also on the faces of people goin' by I see friends shaking hands saying, "How do you do" They're really saying "I love you" I hear babies cry, I watch them grow They'll learn much more than I'll ever know; And I think to myself, What a wonderful world; Yes, I think to myself, What a wonderful world"
                                                                —Louis Armstrong

Photo courtesy of Paul Moody

Photo courtesy of Remy Omar

When people come to fill out an application to work at our nursery, we ask them to share something of themselves with us, something that reflects where they find joy in life. Folks have written poems, submitted beautiful montages of their photographic work, and offered original art pieces. While we cannot offer everyone a job in our small nursery, we get to meet some extraordinary human beings. No person is uninteresting. A young woman wrote us a beautiful piece that introduced us to the Hebrew word "dayenu."* We fell in love with this word and talked about it with everyone we knew—rabbis, lay people, gardeners, and friends. The young woman used it in the context of describing the things that bring her joy and ending each description with "Dayenu." (That would have been enough, but, wait, there's more.) And yes, indeed, there's always more. We can remember incidents or moments that were so perfect, however small, that if we had been struck by lightening in the next moment, we would have lived the most joyous, perfect lives on the planet. Silly, small moments. Dancing in the fading daylight to a John Denver song. Sitting around a campfire in our backfields with old and new friends who had come to celebrate the Harmonic Convergence. Looking at a sky chock full of stars we had never seen before.

And more, there is always more. The universe will continue, no doubt, as it was meant to.

Photo courtesy of Carolyn Heathcote

"When it's over, I want to say: all my life I was a bride married to amazement. I was the bridegroom, taking the world into my arms."
— Mary Oliver

"If the only prayer you said in your whole life was "thank you" that would suffice."

—Meister Eckhart

"When you realize how perfect everything is you will tilt your head back and laugh at the sky." Buddha. *Courtesy of Lucas Foglia Photography*

    * "Dayenu" is a Hebrew song usually sung during Passover. It essentially means, "It would have been enough" and is used to express gratitude for gifts bestowed on the Israelites. Each gift would have been enough. But, wait, there are more.

    "Therefore, how much more so do we owe abundant thanks to God for all the manifold good He bestows upon us? He brought us out of Egypt; He executed justice upon the Egyptians and their gods. He slew their first-born. He gave to us their wealth. He split the sea for us, led us through it on dry land and drowned our oppressors in it. He provided for our needs in the wilderness for forty years and fed us the Manna. He gave us Shabbat, led us to Mount Sinai and gave us the Torah. He brought us into the Land of Israel and built for us the Temple to atone for all our mistakes."

And In The End

So what makes a garden a place of tranquility and sanctuary? In our humble opinion? Anything that makes you laugh, feel peaceful, proud, in awe, at home, have an "aha" moment, or feel connected to anything beyond the mundane. Sure, water and rocks and fragrant plants are magical elements for many of us. But want to add a plastic flamingo? Go ahead!

Peak District, England. *Photo courtesy of Alan & Elizabeth Taylor*

Charlotte, North Carolina.
Photo courtesy of Liz Kearley

Waikoloa, Hawaii. *Photo courtesy of Bill Adams*

Hastings Park. Vancouver, Canada. *Photo courtesy of Mike Wong*

Well, he IS the *king*. Charlotte, North Carolina. *Photo courtesy of Liz Kearley*

Sheila, a photographer from Arizona, shared some dreamy pictures of her grandmother's garden in Missouri. They made us laugh, and laughing is a highly prized activity for us. She said, *"My mother and grandma always had really beautiful gardens. They spent all their extra time nurturing this other world bursting with religious statues, plastic birds, life-size animals, and birdhouses abundant with flowers and plants. My daydreaming still gets the better of me and I visualize, that when no one is looking, the gardens and lawn ornaments come to life. I give them names, feelings, stories, and imagine them interacting with their surroundings. I picture their special kingdom alive with personality."* Truth be told, so do we! Missouri. *Pinhole photos courtesy of Sheila Bocchine*

Bibliography

Bloom, William. *Devas. Fairies and Angels.* Glastonbury, Somerset, England: Gothic Image Publications, 1986.

Clifford, Derek. *A History of Garden Design.* New York, New York: Frederick A. Praeger, Inc., 1963.

Hawken, Paul. *The Magic of Findhorn.* New York, New York: Harper and Row, 1975.

Shaudys, Phyllis. *Growing Fragrant Herbs for Profit.* Washington Crossing, Pennsylvania: Pine Row Publications, 1981.

Small Wright, Machaelle. *Behaving as if the God in All Life Mattered.* Jeffersonton, Virginia: Perelandra, Ltd., 1983.

Photo courtesy of Michael Oberman